CW00404438

Hg2 Miami

A Hedonist's guide to
Miami

BY Charles Froggatt
PHOTOGRAPHY Charles Froggatt

A Hedonist's guide to Miami

Managing director – Tremayne Carew Pole
Marketing director – Sara Townsend
Series editor – Catherine Blake
Design – P&M Design
Maps – Richard Hale
Typesetting – Dorchester Typesetting
Repro – PDQ Digital Media Solutions Ltd
Printer – Printed in Italy by Printer Trento srl
Publisher – Filmer Ltd

Email – info@ahedonistsguideto.com
Website – www.ahedonistsguideto.com

First published in the United Kingdom in October 2005 by
Filmer Ltd
47 Filmer Road
London SW6 7JJ

ISBN – 1-905428-01-4

Hg2 Miami

CONTENTS

How to…

A Hedonist's guide to… is broken down into easy to use sections: Sleep, Eat, Drink, Snack, Party, Culture, Shop, Play and Info. In each of these sections you will find detailed reviews and photographs.

At the front of the book you will find an introduction to the city and an overview map, followed by descriptions of the four main areas and more detailed maps. On each of these maps you will see the places that we have reviewed, laid out by section, highlighted on the map with a symbol and a number. To find out about a particular place, simply turn to the relevant section, where all entries are listed alphabetically.

Alternatively, browse through a specific section (e.g. Eat) until you find a restaurant that you like the look of. Next to your choice will be a small coloured dot – each colour refers to a particular area of the city – then simply turn to the relevant map to discover the location.

Updates

Due to the lengthy publishing process and shelf lives of books it is very difficult to keep travel guides up to date – new restaurants, bars and hotels open up all the time, while others simply fade away or just go out of style. What we can offer you are free updates – simply log onto our website www.ahedonistsguideto.com or www.hg2.net and enter your details, answer a relevant question to provide proof of purchase and you will be entitled to free updates for a year from the date that you sign up. This will enable you to have all the relevant information at your fingertips whenever you go away.

In order to help us, if you have any comments or recommendations that you would like to see in the guide in future please feel free to email us at info@ahedonistsguideto.com.

The concept

A Hedonist's guide to… is designed to appeal to a more urbane and stylish traveller. The kind of traveller who is interested in gourmet food, elegant hotels and seriously chic bars – the traveller who feels the need to explore, shop and pamper themselves away from the madding crowd.

Our aim is to give you the inside knowledge of the city, to make you feel like a well-heeled, sophisticated local and to take you to the most fashionable places in town to rub shoulders with the local glitterati.

In today's world work rules our life, weekends away are few and far between, and when we do go away we want to have the most fun and relaxation possible with the minimum of stress. This guide is all about maximizing time. Everywhere is photographed, so before you go you know exactly what you are getting into; choose a restaurant or bar that suits you and your demands.

We pride ourselves on our independence and our integrity. We eat in all the restaurants, drink in all the bars and go wild in the nightclubs – all totally incognito. We charge no one for the privilege of appearing in the guide; every place is reviewed and included at our discretion.

We feel cities are best enjoyed by soaking up the atmosphere and the vibrancy; wander the streets, indulge in some retail relaxation therapy, re-energize yourself with a massage and then get ready to eat like a king and party hard on the stylish local scene.

It is important for you to explore a city on your own terms, while the places reviewed provide definitive coverage in our eyes; one's individuality can never be wholly accounted for. Sometimes if you take a little extra time to wander off our path, then you may just find the truly hidden gem that we missed.

Miami

The days of cocaine-inspired gang warfare and shoot-outs are long gone. In the words of actor and rapper Will Smith, 'Welcome to Miami' – the place he calls his second home. Why does Will have such affection for Miami? The answer is that the city is the party capital of the United States, and is filled with the most eclectic mix of people outside New York.

If you've heard the phrase 'the town that never sleeps' a hundred times before, this is the one time when you should take it seriously. If it's nightclubs, beautiful people, fast cars, big boats and huge egos you are after, you have come to the right place.

But if you were expecting Americana in all its glory, prepare to be disappointed: Miami is a place where you could quite happily get by without speaking a word of English. The city is broken down into many ethnic groups, creating an eclectic Euro–Latin fusion.

Like any city, Miami has various neighbourhoods, but the extent to which they differ is quite staggering. It's hard to believe that Coral Gables, Downtown and Miami Beach (divided into South Beach and Mid Beach) are all contained within one city. Downtown is the financial nerve-centre, Miami Beach is the party capital, and Coral Gables is the quiet, European influenced district.

In the past, Miami's reputation has been tainted by the presence of drug traffickers. The problem stemmed

from the prohibition era when the beachfront became home to gambling, drinking and fornication, a place where nobody took the blindest bit of notice of the law.

Its long beachfront and southern location meant that Miami had direct, clear access to South and Central America, the source's of cocaine and weed, and in the 1980s it became a magnet for drug-runners. Then the drug enforcement agencies cracked down on dealing and deliveries before finally the city began the big clean-up and models and celebrities returned in force. But drugs continued to be a major influence on life in Miami until the 1990s. Films such as Scarface paint a pretty accurate if somewhat glamorized version of how life was.

Today Miami is the target of much investment, both domestic and international, as the city continues to develop its reputation as a financial centre and link between the US and South America and the Caribbean.

But tourism remains one of Miami's top industries, as visitors come from all over the world to sample the sunshine, eat in the restaurants and party in some of the world's top clubs.

SHOP

HIALEAH

SW 27th Avenue

LIBERTY CITY

Airport Expres

MIAMI

Palmetto Expressway

VIRGINIA GARDENS

Dolphin Expressway

Coral Gables

Flagler Street

SW 8th Street

Tamiami Trail

WESTCHESTER

Coral Way

Bird Way

WEST MIAMI

Coral Way

SW 40th Street

SW 37th Avenue

Calle Ocho

Red Road

SOUTH MIAMI

South Dixie Highway

South Bayshore Drive

COCONUT GROVE

Don Shula Expressway

SW 112th Street

Old Cutler Road

PINECREST

SLEEP

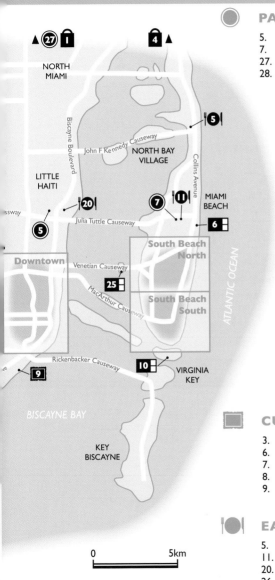

Miami city map

PARTY

5. Grass
7. Jimmy'z
27. Solid Gold
28. Tootsie's Cabaret

CULTURE

3. Bay of Pigs Museum
6. Little Havana
7. Lowe Museum
8. Maximo Gomez Park
9. Vizcaya Museum Gardens

EAT

5. Café Prima Pasta
11. The Forge
20. Ola
26. Romeo's Café

South Beach (North)

According to some Miami locals, this is where East Coast hardcore rapper 50 Cent and his boys were inspired to write the song 'Candy Shop', after a night out drinking champagne in the lounges of South Beach.

If you had to pick one area in Miami in which to be seen looking your finest, then it would be between 14th Street and 22nd Street, where Ocean Drive peters out and Collins Avenue ditches the shops and goes all-out on hotels and party lounges.

This is the epicentre of fashion, dining, parties and a general level of debauchery unmatched anywhere else in America. 'On the Beach' is where the majority of celebs and wannabes do their thing, where the Hummer limos glide menacingly up to the velvet ropes, spilling diamond-clad men and cosmetically enhanced women into the enveloping darkness of yet another VIP lounge.

Mynt, Rok Bar, Sky Bar and Amika are just some of the big name lounges and clubs that typify the area. Glamorous, extravagant and sleek, the clubs are like their clientele. This is where fantasies come true, glam up to the max, bring out your Amex black and lose track of time, your life and your pension plan.

Up this end of South Beach, the hotels are bigger — bigger meaning better in the eyes of

the Miami local. The Setai, the Raleigh, the Shore Club and the Delano are all famous names and cater for those with big budgets. Go for a walk up Collins Avenue and drink at the Art Deco hotel bars, or stroll along the beach and take in the sights of the most exclusive stretch of sand in town.

If Collins is the main artery of this northern part of South Beach, then Lincoln Road is the heartbeat, and the place to find the best shops, restaurants, bars and nightclubs; the most interesting parts of this out-

door mall are between Washington Avenue and Alton Road, where people-watching has become a competitive art form.

For lovers of Hispanic culture, look no further than Española Way. There you will find a crowded little gem of a street packed with restaurants. Most of them can be ignored, but some are popular with Spanish locals who love their tapas and *vino tinto*.

The north of South Beach area ends on the border of what is considered to be Mid Beach. As a rule of thumb, there's no real need to go further north than this point unless you are going to play golf, looking for a quiet spot on the beach, or require a hotel that's off the beaten track. Otherwise South Beach is the reason why most people go to Miami.

CULTURE

1. Art Center South Florida
2. Bass Art Museum
4. Britto Central
5. Holocaust Memorial

EAT

2. Barton G
3. Blue Door (Delano)
7. Casa Tua
18. Nobu (Shore Club)
21. One Ninety
23. Osteria del Teatro
24. Pacific Time
30. Sushi Samba Dromo
32. Touch

PARTY

1. Amika
3. Cafeteria Lounge
4. Crobar
9. Mynt
17. Rumi
19. Tantra
20. Crème
21. Jade Lounge
22. Laundry Bar
24. Score
26. Club Madonna

SHOP

Lincoln Road

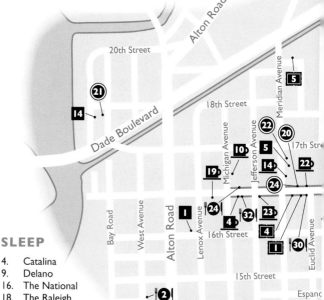

SLEEP

4. Catalina
9. Delano
16. The National
18. The Raleigh
19. Ritz Carlton
20. Sagamore
23. The Setai
24. The Shore Club
26. The Townhouse

South Beach (North) local map

South Beach (South)

Tell someone you're off to Miami, and they'll probably assume that you're heading for South Beach, or SoBe as it is affectionately known locally. It's a magnet for hedonists, and without it Miami would not be known as the exciting city that it is today.

South Beach is a small area of Miami that's detached from the mainland, but which is nevertheless the heartbeat of the city. Its Art Deco landscape is a product of the 1930s and '40s and was constructed after a hurricane demolished much of the beachfront city in 1926. The architects who rebuilt the community were given licence to create whatever they liked, and the result is an abundance of multicoloured, four-storey Art Deco buildings.

More than 800 of these Art Deco buildings still survive on South Beach and the area was protected, in 1979, by the National Register of Historic Places. Most surprising, however, is that the beach, like many things in Miami, is actually fake, created by sand dredged from the sea bed being dumped onto the shoreline. Fake or not, the sand, edged by turquoise water, provides a wonderful canvas for some of the prettiest sunbathers in the world.

If you want a clearer understanding of the place before you get here, just imagine the most louche and artificial arena possible and then fill it

with beautiful people from all over the world who have come to show off their wealth and to party. If you go expecting culture and sophistication, then you'll be disappointed. Here money and fame rule, glamour and glitz are the order of the day and, as long as you accept that, then South Beach can be a lot of fun.

Apart from being one of the longest beaches in America, SoBe is renowned for its hotels, restaurants, nightclubs and shops. It's rather like a grown-up summer camp, except that the sun always shines on South Beach and the party never seems to stop.

South Beach's geography is pretty simple: everywhere you'll ever need to go is within three parallel blocks from the beach. Tourist-packed Ocean Drive is the Art Deco drive set back from the beach, with its multitude of cafés and overpriced and understyled hotels that line the front. Behind that is Collins Avenue – home to the glamour and overstated elegance of some of Miami's finest hotels Finally comes Washington Avenue, grittier, edgier and dirtier, offering an alternative and slightly seedier take on SoBe's playboy paradise.

This area of South Beach is quieter and more residential than the northern part. In actual beach terms, the southern end of South Beach is occupied by surfers and the ultra toned Latino crowd. It is slightly less crowded at this end, but it's where many of the few true Miami locals like to go to escape the tourists.

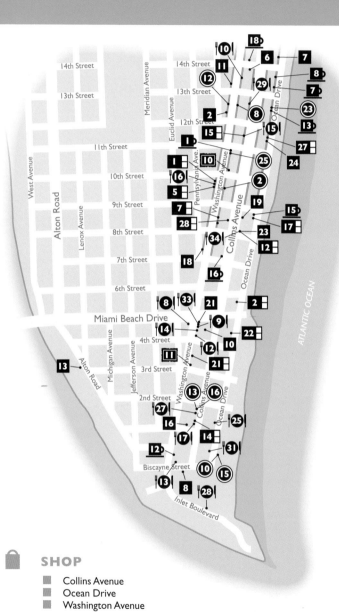

SHOP

- Collins Avenue
- Ocean Drive
- Washington Avenue

PARTY

2. B.E.D.
8. Mansion
10. Nikki Beach
12. Onda Lounge
13. Opium Garden
15. Pearl
16. Privé
23. Palace
25. Twist

SNACK

1. 11th Street Diner
7. Cardozo Café
8. Cavalier
12. Joe's Take Out
13. Leslie Café
15. Pelican Café
16. Puerto Sagua
18. Le Sandwicherie

SLEEP

1. Astor Hotel
2. The Bentley
5. Chelsea Hotel
7. Clinton Hotel
12. The Hotel
14. Mercury Resort
15. Nash Hotel
17. The Pelican
21. St. Augustine
22. The Savoy
27. Victor Hotel
28. Whitelaw Hotel

CULTURE

10. Wolfsonian-FIU
11. Ziff Jewish Museum

EAT

8. China Grill
9. L'Entrecôte de Paris
10. Escopazzo
12. Harrison's Steak House
13. Joe's Stone Crab
14. La Locanda
15. Mark's (Nash Hotel)
16. Metro Kitchen (Astor Hotel)
17. Nemo
25. Prime One Twelve
27. Shoji Sushi
28. Smith & Wollensky
29. Spiga
31. Taverna Opa
33. Tuscan Steak
34. Wish (The Hotel)

DRINK

2. Automatic Slims
6. Club Deuce
7. Finnegan's Way
8. Flute Champagne Bar
10. Harrison's
11. Jazid
13. Monty's
16. The Room
18. Royal Bar
19. Safari Bar
21. Sofi Lounge
23. Tiffany Spire Bar (The Hotel)
24. Vue (The Victor)

Downtown

If you have always wanted to know what 'Downtown' really meant but have been too embarrassed to ask, Miami will clear this up for you. Come to Downtown Miami and you'll find the financial centre, a separate entity that is really only occupied during the day by besuited office folk.

Architecturally, Downtown Miami boasts one of the most impressive skylines in the United States, with rows of skyscrapers and the Four Seasons poking its shiny tinted glass head above the bank of towers, all set against a backdrop of shimmering blue water. To take in the view at its finest, book in at the Mandarin Oriental and sip a glass of champagne on your balcony as the sun goes down.

However, many would say that, like its grand appearance, Downtown is best enjoyed from a distance. Indeed, it's not the shiny modern landscape that it appears to be. It can seem like a ghost town, with a few lunchtime bars for businessmen and an array of electronic stores and immigration houses. Businessmen in the towers stay above ground level during office hours, and then jump into the elevator to the subterranean car park and drive home when the working day is over. Some might venture out on a Friday to the Mandarin's hip 'Barefoot at the Oasis' beach party.

The bad news about Downtown Miami is that if you take a wrong turn, you could find yourself in serious trouble. But the good news is

that this is changing as investors pump cash into the area in the hope that the shopping malls and restaurants will follow. The much anticipated Performing Arts Center is seen as the catalyst for the Downtown face lift and the increasng number of posh apartment buildings that are under construction mean that the Downtown Miami renaissance is serious.

In terms of nightlife, Downtown is where it's at: it's South Florida's answer to Ibiza, and home to two of the largest nightclubs for house and trance music in the state. Nocturnal and Space are super-clubs that bring in top-name international DJs for their all-night sessions. South Beach nightclub owners, having revelled in their sense of security for almost a decade, are now taking mental notes that Downtown is quietly catching up with its 24-hour liquor licences.

Just outside the financial district is the Design District, an area that is becoming noted for its partying – the rapidly devloping nefarious reputation of Pawn Shop, a favourite with the 'more money than sense crowd', and Grass – one of the area's new hotspots.

If you're on business here, note that the Four Seasons, Conrad and Mandarin Oriental hotels are highly rated and have considerably boosted the profile of the district; the Mandarin Oriental is incredibly popular with the glitterati and the wealthier tourists. The Mandarin's restaurant, Azul, is one of the finest in the city; the delicious food is set off by one of the best views in Miami and is definitely worth a dinner.

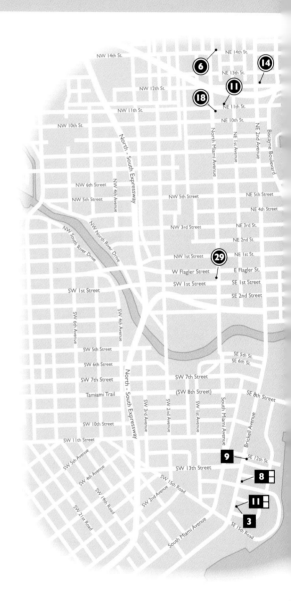

PARTY

6. I/O Lounge
11. Nocturnal
14. Pawn Shop
18. Space
29. Cupid's Cabaret

EAT

1. Azul (Mandarin Oriental)

DRINK

3. Bahia (Four Seasons)
9. Gordon Biersch Brewery
12. M-Bar (Mandarin Oriental)

SLEEP

8. Conrad Hotel
11. The Four Seasons
13. Mandarin Oriental

| 0 | 0.5 | 1km |

Coral Gables

Coral Gables is very different from the other districts: lush green parks and golf clubs are nested away between quiet streets lined by detached coral stone houses with terracotta roofs and inhabited by the rich, who have the local Cubans (Little Havana is found just to the east of here) wash their cars and mow their lawns.

Hedonists may be disappointed: Coral Gables is the tranquil part of town and not a place for parties. In fact it was designed by George Merrick, along with uncle and artist Denman Fink and landscaper Frank Button, in the 1920s in an effort to create the perfect surroundings to bring up their families in a planned community.

With fountains and archways, plaza-like crossroads, streets named Ponce De Leon and Aragon Street, and Spanish hacienda architecture, they gave Coral Gables – the safe, respectable neighbourhood of Miami – a truly European flavour.

Set over 12 square miles, Coral Gables has one major artery, Coral Way. Locally known as Miracle Mile, it runs from east to west in a stretch that is around half a mile long and packed with shops, businesses and restaurants.

So why visit Coral Gables?

Although the majority of the neighbourhood is residential, Coral Gables is also host to almost 200 international companies, so if you are in town on business, there is a good chance that you'll be spending some time here. For shopping, there are some quality little

boutique stores along Coral Way, as well as the George Merrick Village, an up-and-coming designer mall whose European influence is shown in the quieter and more selective range of stores.

Most importantly, Coral Gables is considered the food capital of Florida and boasts some high-quality restaurants. Although they're not renowned for their atmosphere, in culinary terms they are generally superior to the restaurants on South Beach and Downtown. You may fancy heading over to Coral Gables for an early dinner before returning to Downtown or South Beach for the bright lights.

Try the excellent fresh Latin American flavours of Cacao, the Italian-Carribean fusion served at Caramelo or the distinctive flavours of perennial Coral Gables favourite Norman's.

Unless you have a particular fondness for sleepy suburbs, staying in Coral Gables probably won't be very tempting. Golfers, however, should not forget the Biltmore – which not only boasts an 18-hole golf course but also the biggest pool in the continental United States. The hotel's Courtyard Cafe offers a wonderful lunch in the middle of the day and a quiet dinner in the evening.

If South Beach's constant fashion parade gets just a little too much for you, an afternoon lounging by the pool at the Biltmore, followed by a little shopping at Merrick Village before a quiet dinner at Norman's, might just save you.

0   250   500m

 EAT

    4.   Cacao
    6.   Caramelo
  19.   Norman's
  22.   Ortanique on the Mile

 SNACK

    6.   Café Abracci
    9.   Courtyard Grill

SLEEP

    3.   Biltmore Hotel

SHOP

    5.   Village of Merrick Park

sleep...

In Miami your choice of accommodation is your calling-card, so it is worth spending that little bit extra if you intend to look the part. Put simply, the more you spend, the more luxurious your bedroom, the better the hotel spa, the bigger the swimming pool and the closer to the beach you will be. That said, don't worry – in all the hotels listed here, you will be satisfied with what you get. So how do you choose?

Location is obviously important. The majority of big hotels on South Beach are on Collins Avenue and Ocean Drive, but there are some excellent boutique hotels scattered around as well. On Collins Avenue, the Setai, the Raleigh, the Delano, the National, the Sagamore, the Ritz Carlton, the Shore Club and the Savoy all have garden gates at the end of their pool areas with direct access onto the beach. Technically the Victor, the Pelican and the Bentley on Ocean Drive also have access to the beach, but Ocean Drive is set too far back to call itself properly beachside. Of course you'll also want to be close to the bars and restaurants. The Ritz Carlton, the Sagamore, the Delano and the National are all central, as are the Nash, The Hotel and the Whitelaw.

If you've chosen Miami as your destination, a cool pool will probably be high on your wish list. All of the big-budget hotels have luxurious pool areas, while there are some quirky hotels, such as the Bentley or The Hotel, which have

dreamy rooftop pools. There are some excellent hotels – for example, the Townhouse – that do not have pools but do have access to the pools of other hotels.

Only a very good hotel would draw you away from South Beach. The Biltmore Hotel is the jewel in Coral Gables' crown. This is a grand, luxurious old hotel that should not be overlooked, especially by golf lovers. Although there is no beach on the doorstep, there is an 18-hole golf course.

For businessmen staying Downtown, look no further than the Four Seasons or the Conrad, as these two tower blocks cater for even the most picky tycoon, while sitting on its own island and overlooking the Downtown skyline from Brickell Key is the Mandarin Oriental, one of the top hotels in Miami. If conven-

ience is paramount, go for the Four Seasons or the Conrad, but for virtually unrivalled luxury choose the Mandarin Oriental, which is as much for holiday-makers as it is for businessmen.

At the other end of the scale, there are some interesting options. Low profile, economical, but stylish hotels are becoming more popular in Miami. The St Augustine and the Whitelaw are two examples: they haven't joined the Miami hotel rat race by raising their prices and they still retain their own charm. These are both afford-able hotels that would still manage to satisfy the super-rich and famous.

The rates quoted here are for a standard double in low season and a one-bed-room suite in high season. All hotels are assessed for style, atmosphere and location.

Our top ten hotels in Miami are:
1. The Setai
2. Raleigh $325
3. Shore Club
4. Mandarin Oriental
5. Sagamore 3+
6. Fisher Island Club
7. Delano
8. Biltmore
9. The Hotel
10. Pelican

Our top five hotels for style are:
1. Raleigh
2. The Setai
3. Shore Club
4. Mandarin Oriental
5. Sagamore

Our top five hotels for atmosphere are:
1. Shore Club
2. Raleigh
3. Delano
4. The Setai
5. Whitelaw

Our top five hotels for location are:
1. Ritz Carlton
2. Sagamore
3. Bentley
4. The Hotel
5. Savoy

Astor Hotel, 956 Washington Avenue, South Beach
Tel: 305 531 8081 www.hotelastor.com
Rates: $140–750

The Astor Hotel is a stop on South Beach's Art Deco bus tour.
Designed by architect T. Hunter Henderson in 1936 and renovated in 1997 and 2002, the Astor is a stylish hotel that loves to
show off on Tuesdays by hosting a party at the hip Metro bar
beside its lobby. Next to the Chelsea on Washington Avenue, the
Astor has given the road a bit of a face-lift with a neatly kept
hedgerow and garden in front of the building's coral stone
façade. The lobby's marble flooring and solid square wooden
table ooze taste, and the 40 rooms, standard for a building of
this period, are made to look inviting with blond oak wood
headboards and beds dressed in Frette cotton sheets. The staff
are helpful and devoted to ensuring the privacy of 'special'
clients. The Astor is the most stylish of the boutique hotels in
Miami, and it takes its image very seriously.

Style 9, Atmosphere 8, Location 7

Bentley Hotel, 510 Ocean Drive, South Beach
Tel: 305 538 1700 www.thebentleyhotels.com
Rates: $220–1,200

The Bentley is a no-nonsense hotel. It sits on Ocean Drive a couple of doors down from TGI Fridays, but remains almost unnoticed by the masses that walk by. From top to bottom the Bentley is an attractive option for a weekend away: the rooftop pool and jacuzzi have uninterrupted views of the beach, with a large deck meant solely for sunbathing and drinking, while in the bedroom the Bentley performs well with elevated beds, kitchen areas and sofas. In fact you can rent a room all year round here. Try to book a room with a sea view or balcony, otherwise you'll end up overlooking a small but plain courtyard. The Bentley attracts the kind of client that has a substantial amount of cash in the bank but does not feel the need to tell the world about it, and thus adds a touch of class to Ocean Drive.

Style 9, Atmosphere 7/8, Location 8

Biltmore Hotel, 1200 Anastasia Avenue, Coral Gables
Tel: 305 445 1926 www.biltmorehotel.com
Rates: $159–2,850

At 21,000 square foot, the Biltmore's pool is the largest in the continental United States, and used to be the domain of Johnny Weissmuller, who later became Tarzan. The hotel itself is the creation of Coral Gables' founder George Merrick and John McEntee in 1925, and architecturally it could be a thousand miles away from South Beach, not a 20-minute drive. Your first walk through the lobby will take your breath away: with its hand-painted vaulted ceilings, 25-foot columns, oversized arches, porcelain planters, French and Spanish furniture, marble floors and oriental rugs, it looks more like a mosque in Granada. The building's bell tower, modelled after the Giralda bell tower in Seville, is 300 feet high. During Word War II it served as a hospital, and people say that ghosts of soldiers and even Al Capone, after whom the Everglades Suite is named, roam the halls here. Bill Clinton, however, stayed in the Al Capone suite and had no problems – as far as we know. Instead he enjoyed the 18-hole golf course.

Style 7/8, Atmosphere 7, Location 5

Catalina Hotel, 1732 Collins Avenue, South Beach
Tel: 305 674 1160 www.southbeachgroup.com
Rates: from $75

The Catalina is the latest addition to the South Beach Group's hotel empire, of which this, the Chelsea, the Mercury and the Whitelaw are the pick of the bunch. Located in front of the stylish Raleigh Hotel on Collins Avenue, the Catalina can be identified by its large windowed front that looks more like a sportscar showroom. The lobby is a roomy, tranquil space with white curtains flowing down from the double-height ceiling towards a set of white leather mini sofas, crafted wooden stools and an egg-in-a-hole chair. It's very Miami. Apart from the spotty red lampshades, the rooms could not be any whiter, and there is plenty of room for the in-house masseuse to pay guests a visit. Out back there is a 75-foot pool, while the lobby's bar serves free drinks to hotel guests between 7 and 8pm.

Style 8, Atmosphere 9, Location 9

Chelsea Hotel, 944 Washington Avenue, South Beach
Tel: 305 534 4069 www.thehotelchelsea.com
Rates: $95–225

The Chelsea is popular with young professionals, including a loyal set of up-and-coming models, which is probably why the management has named the lobby's bar, the 'Eye Candy Bar'. The feng-shui inspired rooms with bamboo floors and amber lighting are basic but clean, with large and comfortable beds. The Chelsea is not luxurious – it's economical – but stylish enough to attract a handsome crowd that likes to party. The terrace is where you sip coffee in the morning at the same futuristic, metallic tables where you had your first sake the night before. Like the Catalina, Mercury and Whitelaw in the South Beach Group, guests enjoy free drinks for an hour in the evenings, as well as free rides to and from the airport and the deal-clinching complimentary yoga classes. The Chelsea is next door to the Astor Hotel, whose Metro Bar gets packed on a Tuesday.

> **Style 7, Atmosphere 8, Location 7**

Circa 39, 3900 Collins Avenue, Miami Beach
Tel: 305 538 4900 www.circa39.com
Rates: $109–229

This is a cleverly located hotel that was renovated in 2004 and is now one of the dark horses of the Miami hotel industry. It's found 'mid-beach', which is Miami's equivalent of no-man's-land. In holiday terms, this means a beachside hotel within striking distance (about 15 blocks) of South Beach's party zone, but just far enough away from the sound of house music and revved-up Hummer engines to ensure a restful night's sleep. Circa 39 gets

its name from its original construction in 1939, its location on Collins Avenue and 39th Street, and the fact that it was formerly called the Copley Plaza circa 1939. The rates are satisfyingly low for an establishment that offers 86 decently sized rooms (this is a classic Art Deco building so room sizes are all similar), a large pool with massage cabanas and a really stylish bar that is becoming popular with Miami's in-crowd. The beach is a minute's walk away, and the location of the hotel means that there will be acres of free sand.

Style 7, Atmosphere 8, Location 7

Clinton Hotel, 825 Washington Ave, South Beach
Tel: 305 538 1471   www.clintonsouthbeach.com
Rates: from $89

Newly opened in 2004, the Clinton is as boutique as they come. Designed by Frenchman Eric Raffi, the hotel features an extraordinary giant lampshade-shaped sofa in its lobby. Some of the rooms have mini verandas that overlook an enclosed ankle-deep ornamental pool, unique in Miami, while others watch over the courtyard pool area. The en-suite bathrooms all have large windows looking into the bedrooms over the basins so that lovers need not lose eye contact while they floss. Outside, in the slightly cramped courtyard, guests can swim against the tide in the exercise pool or float quietly in a still water pool. The hotel also

offers other services that include guaranteeing entry to all Miami nightclubs, picking up guests' shopping… and offering 'dream therapy' (just push a button on your phone to reach one of the 'dream specialists'). If you are a shopaholic, like to party and don't mind a small pool, then the Clinton is the place to be.

Style 7, Atmosphere 7, Location 7

Conrad Hotel, 1395 Brickell Avenue, Downtown
Tel: 305 503 6500 www.conradhotels.com
Rates: $159–319

The Espirito Santo Plaza building that houses the Conrad Hotel is unquestionably the sexiest of all buildings in the Downtown area. The 36-storey structure is built of concave glass and has an 11-floor atrium on the 25th floor that contains the Conrad's lobby, restaurant and lounge. The Conrad is the luxury brand of the Hilton chain and has 203 rooms and 103 serviced residences. The rooms are decorated with contrasting elements of glass, wood, leather and metal, matching the building's style, and include remote-control lighting, a pillow menu and a whole host of gadgets. The hotel has its own spa, but most importantly has the Noir Bar beside the Sky Lobby that offers the best views of Biscayne Bay. If the Noir Bar gets quiet, use one of the telescopes in the lobby to see whether the Bahia Bar beside the Four Seasons' pool area is full.

Delano Hotel, 1685 Collins Avenue, South Beach
Tel: 305 672 2000 www.delanohotelmiamibeach.com
Rates: $375–1,175

The Delano has appeared in more brochures than any other hotel on the Beach and is firmly established as a Miami landmark. However, the buzz in the cocktail lounges and beauty salons of South Beach is that the Delano has lost its touch. The reason why the Delano is not as cool as it used to be is because it is so spectacular. If it weren't for the Alice in Wonderland theme, if it didn't have such a breathtaking lobby, if Ian Schrager didn't have the reputation that he does today for making such inspired hotels, and if the pool didn't have underwater music, then there would be no tourists walking around the premises taking photos, and that edge of exclusivity would still be talked about between cosmopolitans and botox injections. It sounds strange, but the

Delano was just too good a hotel to remain cool for long. But that's Miami. On arrival, guests are escorted through the famous lobby, with its huge pillars and billowing curtains, up to one of the 208 crisp white rooms. After arrival, head to the Aqua Spa for a massage, have a drink at the lobby's Rose Bar, check out the poolside bungalows and stick your head in the water to hear Beethoven's Third Symphony.

Fisher Island Club, I Fisher Island Drive, Fisher Island
Tel: 305 535 6020 www.fisherisland-florida.com
Rates: $325–2,040

In 1919 developer Carl Fisher swapped his yacht *Eagle* for
William Vanderbilt's 216-acre winter island estate. Fisher Island
has become home to a community of 1920s-style villas and can
be reached by helicopter, ferry, rowing boat, submarine or whatever other mode of transport the celebrities on the island
choose. The hotel offers villa suites, cottages or seaside villas, but
all have views of Biscayne Bay and the Downtown Miami skyline.
This is as private as it gets in Miami. The resort has its own
beach, tennis courts, golf course, spa and salon, and the idea is to
enjoy the facilities out of the view of the general public. In addition to hot tubs, guests are given golf buggies to travel around
the island. There is a high-quality restaurant in the Vanderbilt
Mansion and there's also the Beach Club and Sunset Bar, while
South Beach's nightlife is still within easy reach.

Style 9/10, Atmosphere 8, Location 6

Four Seasons, 1435 Brickell Avenue, Downtown
Tel: 305 358 3535 www.fourseasons.com
Rates: $275–4,000

With 70 floors, the Four Seasons hotel and Towers building is the tallest on the Miami skyline and is visible from South Beach. Many of the Four Seasons' guests are on business, but at weekends a good proportion book in on vacation. Like the Ritz Carlton, guests know pretty much what to expect – except at this Four Seasons, giant Buddha-like statues stand in the building's main lobby as well as in the hotel's lobby, where the paintings of Latin American artists hang. The rooms all include king-size beds, as one would expect, but also feature padded windowsills so that guests can look over Biscayne Bay and beyond in comfort. There are 221 rooms, including 39 suites in the hotel, and the pool area occupies two acres in which the guests can recline and sip on a cocktail. The resident Italian restaurant Aqua is well rated, but the biggest plus point for this hotel is the Bahia Bar, which lures in the fashionable crowd and gives a predominately business-like atmosphere a kick up the ass.

Style 7, Atmosphere 7, Location 6

The Hotel, 801 Collins Avenue, South Beach
Tel: 305 531 2222 www.thehotelofsouthbeach.com
Rates: $195–425

The Hotel was built in 1939 by L. Murray Dixon, the man who designed many of the buildings in the area, but was redecorated in 1998 by clothing designer Todd Oldham. This was formerly the Tiffany Hotel, but although it lost the right to keep the name it retained the 'Tiffany Spire'. The octagonal pool is the most stylish roof pool in Miami, with clear views of the Atlantic and the Miami skyline. There is a separate bar around the spire and a second in the lobby, and the hotel's resident restaurant, Wish, highly rated in Miami, produces excellent scallops. What does raise a few eyebrows, however, is the clinical lime, apple-green and blue finish to the hotel's interior. People in Miami do go on about how stylish it is, but it can be rather stark and cold. Unfortunately the staff are made to wear matching tie-dye shirts that make even the Germans look stylish.

Style 7/8, Atmosphere 9, Location 10

Mandarin Oriental, 500 Brickell Key Drive, Downtown
Tel: 305 913 8288   www.mandarinoriental.com
Rates: $575–5,000

Built on Brickell Key for over $100 million, the Mandarin Oriental is a luxurious 44-acre island overlooking Miami's financial district. Not just a hotel, the Mandarin Oriental has added a 20,000-foot white sand beach club, complete with beds adorned with white cushions and canopies, beach butlers and beachside cabana treatments – as if the three-storey spa wasn't enough. The rooms, many of which have balconies overlooking the water, were designed by Hirsch Bedner & Associates, and feature high ceilings, king-size beds and opulent Spanish marble bathrooms with separate bath tubs and showers. Downstairs, the Azul restaurant and the Martini bar (with over 100 different Martinis) are both popular with Miami's hip scene, so guests could happily stay at the hotel for a week without leaving the island. South Beach's lounges are just a 10-minute drive away, but the Mandarin's own take on the party scene kicks into action on a Friday night and is a good starting-point.

Style 9/10, Atmosphere 9, Location 5

Mercury Resort, 100 Collins Avenue, South Beach
Tel: 305 398 3000 www.mercuryresort.com
Rates: $165–995

The Mercury has three things going for it. First, it is adjoined to the Shoji Sushi and Nemo restaurants, both of which are excellent and provide room service. Second, the hotel's pool area is itself joined onto a surf shop and surfers' sandwich shack. Third, it is located just yards away from Opium and Privé nightclubs, so lazy weekenders do not have to walk very far to find what they need. And if you're a fitness freak there's a fourth: you have to walk a block and a half to the beach. The hotel itself is not particularly high-tech, but it does have a shiny light wood finish to it and the rooms include spacious bathrooms with spa tubs (with the duplex suites being particularly good value out of season). The Mercury is therefore ideal for a weekend break for the self-professed bone-idle traveller.

Style 7, Atmosphere 9, Location 8

Nash Hotel, 1120 Collins Avenue, South Beach
Tel: 305 674 7800 www.hotelnash.com
Rates: $155–525

In Miami, hotel owners are often left with two choices: either they develop a stylish hotel and hire a PR company to lure in the fickle Miami crowd, or they target a more sophisticated and discriminating clientele who book fewer rooms but are better news in the long run. At the Nash they opted for the latter, offering a more tranquil experience than their immediate competitors. This is a quiet, stylish and well-located hotel, a block behind the infamous Versace mansion in the nerve-centre of the Art Deco district, which is packed with shops, bars and nightclubs. Guests are greeted in the Nash's smooth lobby area at a Gucci-inspired wooden desk before being shown to one of the 54 rooms that have been done up in soothing sage and ivory, and furnished with shield-shaped armoires and lounge beds. The courtyard garden has three small spa pools as its centrepiece:

fresh, salt and mineral water. The hotel's resident restaurant is Mark's, which, like the Nash, produces top results without the fuss of the Miami crowd. A stylish hotel that dislikes the gritty Miami attitude that attracts the A-list.

Style 9, Atmosphere 6, Location 10

National, 1677 Collins Avenue, South Beach
Tel: 305 532 8370   www.nationalhotel.com
Rates: $270–480

Parked beside the Delano on Collins Avenue, this yellow Art Deco classic looks the part with a stunning 205-foot 'infinity' pool and its own furniture on the beach; and it talks the talk

with a French restaurant, a lobby cocktail bar called 'D' Lounge' and a poolside bar called 'Zee pool Lounge'. These names may sound German when read aloud, but nevertheless ze National is making an effort to fit in. Whatever the hotel's accent, Miami locals judge hotels by their lobby and the National's stark hallway has been found wanting by the in-crowd, which means D' Lounge is only occupied by residents. Apart from the three-storey penthouse suite, the rooms here are bland and badly upholstered; but the good news is that the National has 32 ultra-modern poolside cabanas that feature flat-screen TVs, European linen and feather pillows. The hotel is well-equipped for functions of all kinds, and attracts a mixed crowd of businessmen and large groups of friends who have come to live it large on D' beach.

Style 7, Atmosphere 6/7, Location 9

Pelican, 826 Ocean Drive, South Beach
Tel: 305 673 3373 www.pelicanhotel.com
Rates: $135–440

South Beach's only toy-hotel, The Pelican is Diesel's first hotel venture, featuring 30 themed rooms in the style of the fashion company's advertising campaigns. Quite when the 'Me Tarzan, you Vain' campaign came out, nobody really knows. Designed by Swede Magnus Ehrlad, the rooms are decorated with original furnishings from the '30s to the '70s and are given names such as

'Born in the Stars & Stripes' and 'Psychedelic(ate) Girl'; the most popular is Room 212, which is named 'Best Little Whorehouse'. The Pelican's downfall is that it does not have a pool, but it does provide private sun-loungers on the beach. There is, however, an eight-person jacuzzi in the $2,500-a-night penthouse, which has three bedrooms and looks like a porn-star's palace. The main room is overlooked by a circular tropical fish tank six feet across, which is embedded in a $17,000 copper wall.

Style 9, Atmosphere 8, Location 8

The Raleigh, 1775 Collins Avenue, South Beach
Tel: 305 534 6300   www.raleighhotel.com
Rates: $150–1,095

Hardly advertised, but always talked about. With its entrance secluded behind palm trees and hedges, The Raleigh feels like the gentle giant of the strip: giant, because it boasts one of the largest, sexiest pools on South Beach as well as an enclosed beach area for full-moon parties. And gentle because, well, you just don't feel like you are on show here and the hotel only has 104 rooms, ensuring that guests can relax in style rather than fighting for the sun beds, hammocks and love dens. The rooms are spacious, boast terrazzo floors, cedar-wood furniture and king-size beds, are fully equipped with all the standard issue mod-cons and have walk-in showers big enough for a small

cheerleading team. Here the aim is not to be pampered by hundreds of waiters, but to enjoy attentive service at a distance; likewise with the regular photo shoots and catwalks around the pool. The Sunday pool party is an all-day session that is legendary. This is one of the most stylish hotels in Miami, attracting the most stylish guests.

Style 10, Atmosphere 10, Location 9

Ritz Carlton, 1 Lincoln Road, South Beach
Tel: 786 276 4000 www.ritzcarlton.com
Rates: from $239

Apart from the long sandy beach full of half-naked people on the hotel's doorstep, this Ritz Carlton feels a lot like any other Ritz Carlton around the world. It's big, it's impersonal, it's luxurious and you know exactly what you're going to get. It was formerly the DiLido until $200 million was poured into refurbishing it, resulting in the smartest hotel on the beach – smart being something South Beach is not renowned for. Here the elevator music is as one would imagine elevator music to be (not techno or the latest Ibiza chill-out mix); the rooms are impeccably presented, feature king-size beds and antique furniture (not retro stools and transparent tables); and the staff are polite but too formal for SoBe. Much of the money spent on this building appears to have gone into the hotel's enormous and impressive

lobby, as well as its pool area, which has been designed to look like the deck of a luxury cruise liner overlooking the Ocean. This is an impressive hotel where guests pay for the service and the guarantee that their stay will go smoothly.

Style 7, Atmosphere 7/8, Location 10

Sagamore, 1671 Collins Avenue, South Beach
Tel: 305 535 8088 www.sagamorehotel.com
Rates: $215–1,050

Another hotel that gets top marks for style is the Sagamore. A cross between an art gallery and a hotel, the Sagamore oozes quality, but, unlike the Delano or the Shore Club, does not feel the need to tell people about it. Instead they like to show art, and lots of it. The Sagamore boasts the largest contemporary art collection of all the hotels on the Beach, and displays it in all the public areas, including the lobby (where metallic sculptures made out of dustbins greet guests). Built in 1948 by local architect Albert Anis, but restored in 2001, the Sagamore is an example of post-modern Miami architecture that has strayed slightly from the area's traditional Art Deco style. The hotel houses 93 rooms – or suites, to be more accurate. Each has its own kitchen, is equipped with functional, modernist furniture, and has oversized windows. Outside guests can enjoy the L-shaped pool framed by a well-kept lawn and an efficient team of waiters who attend to your every need.

St Augustine, 347 Washington Avenue, South Beach
Tel: 305 532 0570
Rates: $145–175

This discreet gem south of 5th Street is a cross between a spa, art gallery and hotel, and is ideal for couples that do not plan to leave the building. The rooms are designed like cosmopolitan lofts, with large maple-wood beds that look as if they are floating because of an elevated step at the foot. Rooms are fully kitted out with electronic fittings, as well as boasting some well-considered mini bars. Even better are the double-sized bathrooms that feature glass spa cabinets with multijet spray showers and steam baths, as well as a spa bar with aromatherapy oils, eye masks, body buffs and creams. If you make it back into the lobby, then take a look at the paintings by local artists on display there. They are all for sale, as are cocktails at the hotel's shiny orange-plastic-topped bar with matching stools.

Style 8, Atmosphere 8, Location 7

49

The Savoy, 425 Ocean Drive, South Beach
Tel: 800 215 2167 www.savoymiami.com
Rates: from $129

The Savoy Hotel is the only hotel on Ocean Drive right on the sand with private beach access. It also happens to be a trendy part of the beach popular with surfers and lithe Latino surf bunnies. It spans more than two acres and has two swimming pools encircled by palm trees and tropical foliage and two elevated sunbathing areas that look directly onto the beach. This is the quieter, southern end of Ocean Drive that allows guests to strike at the restaurants and nightclubs nearby and only hear the sound of waves at night (instead of the unrelenting house beats that many hotels have to endure). There are 75 suites at the Savoy, which are simple, tiled rooms with all-white bedding, additional seating areas and kitchens. There is an in-house restaurant, but there are dozens better within walking distance.

Style 6, Atmosphere 7/8, Location 7/8

The Setai, 2001 Collins Avenue, South Beach
Tel: 305 520 6100 www.thesetai.com
Rates: $485–25,000

On South Beach it is easy to get distracted with talk about who is doing what where. For a moment let's forget about who bought the 6,000-square-foot Setai penthouse with a rooftop infinity pool. Let's forget which African American rock star has a recording studio on the seventh floor and let's forget which American cyclist who battled back from illness and won the Tour de France hangs out here. Rather, let's focus on the black granite bathrooms with rainfall showers and oversized bathtubs in the apartments, the Dux beds, the views of the neighbouring hotels and the Miami shoreline from high up on the Setai's tinted glass

rimmed balconies, the Setai's luxurious spa, the Setai's three pools, and the 90-foot outdoor bar. This shiny new 38-storey apartment building is even more stylish than the Mandarin Oriental, is more 'exclusive' than the neighbouring Shore Club, and has more efficient staff than every hotel in Miami. Apart from the $1,000-a-night price tag here, it's hard to pick a weakness in the Setai's armour. So let's just concentrate on the words of one of the ultra-efficient staff who came from Japan to work here: 'The Setai brings new meaning to the word luxury.' He was right. He and the Setai may take a bow.

Style 10, Atmosphere 10, Location 9

The Shore Club, 1901 Collins Avenue, South Beach
Tel: 305 695 3277 www.shoreclub.com
Rates: $345–2,200

While most reports will tell you that The Shore Club is the hottest hotel on the beach, approach Ian Schrager's latest Miami masterpiece with caution. Yes, the Shore Club does have two top-class restaurants in Nobu and Ago; the resident Sky Bar attracts a large number of luscious party animals; the pool areas (one is Olympic-sized and the other is smaller but more exclusive) are flanked with idyllic den areas. There is an ocean-side bungalow designed for Lenny Kravitz, with its own gated pool. The lobby's flowing white curtains lit up around the pillars are very seductive; the staff look good in their white outfits; and the 6,000 square foot, three-storey penthouse is idyllic. But with 322 rooms and 70 suites (designed by British architect David Copperfield), and an additional mass of outsiders looking to eat at the restaurants and party at the Sky Bar (which produces an unending loud chorus of up-to-the-minute beats), understand that the Shore Club is not a hotel from which guests leave as refreshed as they would like to. A relaxing weekend away the Shore Club is not.

Style 9, Atmosphere 9/10, Location 9

The Standard, 40 Island Avenue, Miami Beach
Tel: 305 673 1717 www.standardhotel.com
Rates: $150–750

André Balazs kitsch cult classic comes to Miami in the form of a spa hotel, although die-hard fans of the LA outposts might be a little disappointed by the lack of retro furniture and aspiring actor staff. The Miami Standard promises to be the epitome of holistic well-being focusing on re-energising exhausted hedonists coming to Miami to recharge. Situated on Belle Isle, a landscaped residential island, five minutes from the beach, The Standard is away from the frenetic activity of SoBe. The hotel's private docks and spectacular views provide a moment of tranquillity, but the Garden Fire Lounge still promises one of the best parties.

Style 8/9, Atmosphere 8/9, Location 8

The Townhouse, 150 20th Street, South Beach
Tel: 305 534 3800   www.townhousehotel.com
Rates: $105–350

The Townhouse's strengths revolve around its relaxed atmosphere, its stark minimalist décor, and its roof terrace that makes all others in Miami look shoddy. Nowhere else in Miami is there a jigsaw puzzle in the lobby, and nowhere else can guests sit on swings in the building's porch. The hotel is overshadowed by the fabulous Setai in terms of pure extravagance, but the Townhouse's style is to attract normal mortals who don't need to spend a $1,000 a night in order to taste the best South Beach has to offer. The Bond Street Lounge is the hotel's resident basement bar, but the roof terrace is the place to enjoy an evening beverage, especially on a Friday. The downer is that the Townhouse does not have a pool, but this is when guests should take advantage of the fact that some hotels, including the Raleigh (the Raleigh's lagoon pool is the top trump of Miami pools) welcome visitors to their pools as long as they order plenty of drinks and look good in a bikini. Otherwise there is the beach just 50 yards away.

Style 7, Atmosphere 8, Location 8/9

The Victor Hotel, 1144 Ocean Drive, South Beach
Tel: 305 428 1234 www.hotelvictorsouthbeach.com
Rates: from $350

The Victor opened in February 2005 and set out to attract as many celebs as it possibly could. Before opening, the Hotel Victor hired a 'Vibe Manager', Victoria Prado, to ensure that the in-crowd are happy with the music, the lighting and the smell of the hotel during their stay. This does mean, however, that if you are not famous, they probably won't put on your favourite album for you. According to Prado, cool people like listening to the beat of

artists unknown to the masses, or remixes of 1980s songs. That aside, designer Jacques Garcia, the man behind the Hotel Costes, Paris, and New York's Spice Market, has steered clear of the Miami minimalism and opted for a large boutiquey feel. The Victor has adopted a jellyfish theme, and there is a fascinating aquarium in the lobby, as well as images of jellyfish projected onto the hotel bar's giant screen – but luckily the ultra-stylish rimless pool is free of Portuguese men-of-war (unlike the Miami coastline).

Style 7/8, Atmosphere 8, Location 8/9

Whitelaw Hotel, 808 Collins Avenue, South Beach
Tel: 305 398 7000 www.southbeachgroup.com
Rates: from $89

If your intention is to get as drunk as you possibly can for free in a stylish lobby bar before you go out and party, then this is the place for you – the lobby bar serves free drinks for an hour to guests before they go out. The hotel's motto is 'Clean sheets, hot water and stiff drinks'. The rooms are all in white and as spacious as you'd expect in an Art Deco building such as this. Most of the staff are Hispanic in origin, apart from one female German bartender who serves the tastiest mojito in town, and are ultra-friendly, providing guests with free entrance to many of the clubs. The one drawback to the Whitelaw is that there is no pool, but for around $150 a night, nobody is complaining. Instead guests are given the best seats in the house to watch the homies, rappers, glamour models and other Miami lovers walk by.

Style 7, Atmosphere 9/10, Location 10

eat...

The majority of restaurants mentioned here are on South Beach, but that's just because SoBe is where you'll want to be. If you're serious about your food you'll probably be better off looking at the Downtown and Coral Gables options.

In South Beach *where* you eat and *with whom* you eat can be far more important than *what* you eat. Food critics will try to convince you otherwise, but the undeniable truth is that in South Beach, people pay for the company and the location rather than what is in front of them. The menus offer the most elaborate fusions of flavours and styles known to man, but very often use overdressed vocabulary to disguise something far more simple. Eating out here can be rather like driving a Ferrari with a Skoda engine – try and see through the frills to work out what is really on offer.

With its eclectic mix of cultures, Miami has a wonderfully diverse selection of restaurants, from high-end Italians and modern American cooking to earthier but equally good Cuban, Caribbean and Latin American cuisine.

Seafood is on offer almost everywhere, which is hardly surprising given the city's location, and is second to none in the country. Legendary eatery Joe's Stone Crab prides itself on just one thing, and no prizes for guessing what that may be. To avoid the queue, grab a

take-out and hit the beach with a bucket of crabs and a chilled bottle of Sancerre.

It's quite hard to find somewhere that successfully combines fantastic food with a buzzing atmosphere, but Nobu and One Ninety both manage to pull it off. Elsewhere the likes of Sushi Samba and the Metro Kitchen are all about buzz

and celebrity sightings, with the food seemingly slipping to a disappointing second. Alternatively restaurants such as Wish at The Hotel offer great food but are a little wanting in atmosphere. In terms of service – hey, this is the States! The service is great almost everywhere.

Beyond South Beach, the restaurants we've included tend to be slightly more formal, but the food is often superior. If you head to Downtown check out Azul, in the Mandarin Oriental, with its fantastic views of the city, or the Latin American Ola. If you're intent on sampling Florida's best cooking, make the 15-minute drive from South Beach to Coral Gables. Here the chefs and restaurants take themselves very seriously, so leave your open-collared shirts and tight jeans at home and slip on that blazer.

The restaurants are all rated by food, service and atmosphere and the price given is for two courses for one, with half a bottle of wine.

Our top ten restaurants in Miami are:
1. Nobu
2. Casa Tua
3. Pacific Time
4. Azul
5. One Ninety
6. Shoji Sushi
7. Wish
8. The Forge
9. La Locanda
10. Café Prima Pasta

Our top five restaurants for food are:
1. Nobu
2. One Ninety
3. Pacific Time
4. Casa Tua
5. Azul

Our top five restaurants for service are:
1. Shoji Sushi
2. Wish
3. Azul
4. Casa Tua
5. Pacific Time

Our top five restaurants for atmosphere are:
1. La Locanda
2. Nobu
3. Sushi Samba
4. Metro Kitchen
5. The Forge

Azul, Mandarin Oriental Hotel, 500 Brickell Key Drive, Downtown
Tel: 305 913 8254 www.mandarinoriental.com
Open: midday–3pm and 7–11pm daily $110

Located in the Mandarin Oriental on Brickell Key, Azul is the only restaurant in Miami with views of the Downtown skyline and Biscayne Bay. Sit either on the terrace and enjoy the sound of the waves lapping away at the shore, or inside, soaking up the backdrop through floor-to-ceiling windows and watching the boats glide by. The open marble kitchen is state-of-the-art; from here the very able executive chef Clay Conley creates award-winning fusion dishes cooked to perfection. Sommelier Richard Hales has developed a well-considered wine list that draws the best from the food. Azul oozes sophistication, and its location in such a fashionable hotel gives the restaurant solid credentials for Miami's image-conscious diners. For pre- or post-dinner drinks, M-Bar at the other end of the Mandarin Oriental's lobby boasts an impressive 250 varieties of Martini in its armoury.

Food 9, Service 9, Atmosphere 8

Barton G, 1427 West Avenue, Miami Beach
Tel: 305 672 8881 www.bartong.com
Open: 6–10.30pm (midnight Sat/Sun) daily $90

Before Barton G the restaurant existed, corporations raved about the culinary artistry of event-planner Barton G. Weiss and his over-the-top event productions for Fortune 500 companies. In 2002 he opened Barton G, serving dishes such as Popcorn Shrimp, spilling out of a cinema container onto a bed of real popcorn, or Swordfish served on a sword. The restaurant has been a hit since head chef Ted Mendez arrived and attracts the Miami's big-spenders. Refreshingly located away from the current South Beach hotspots, it's housed in the former Starfish restaurant that featured so heavily in the SoBe renaissance. The onyx bar by the entrance backed by a glass wall of 100 test tubes filled with flowers gives a hint of what's to come. Barton G prides itself on being over-the-top in every department. The atmosphere is relaxed as Miami's hip crowd drink as many cocktails as they can before enjoying a really good supper with a twist of American kitsch.

Food 8, Service 8, Atmosphere 8

Blue Door, Delano Hotel, 1685 Collins Avenue, South Beach
Tel: 305 674 6400   www.delanohotelmiamibeach.com
Open: 11am–4pm, 7–11.30pm daily $100

When Madonna co-owned Blue Door at the Delano, it was almost impossible to book a table. The girls were beautiful, the men were spending obscene amounts of cash and everybody was happy. That was until people realized the food wasn't any good and interest began to wane. Frenchman Claude Troisgros took on the restaurant and now he and executive chef Stephane Becht have restored Blue Door's reputation for fine dining. The menu is steeped in French refinement, while the comprehensive

wine list is just as exclusive as one would expect from such a location. The Blue Door's impressive design continues the Alice and Wonderland theme of the Delano, combining white leather screens, candles and tablecloths and billowing floor-to-ceiling drapery, while the view of the Delano's gardens from the terrace is tranquil. Try stopping off at the Rose Bar for a pre-dinner drink. You may need it while you wait for service.

Food 8, Service 6, Atmosphere 8

Cacao 141 Giralda Avenue, Coral Gables
Tel: 305 445 1001   www.cacaorestaurant.com
Open: 11.30am–3pm, 6–10.30pm (11.30pm Thurs–Sat). Closed
Sat lunch and Sun. $85

From the pavement, this Latin American restaurant looks like most of the restaurants clustered on Giralda Avenue. The interior, however, is sleek; guests sit on soft, orange chairs in a well-lit dining hall with a terracotta floor, with the wine cellar satisfyingly

visible through glass panels in the background. Chef Edgar Leal has a growing reputation for bringing ancient South American cooking to life, and the menu covers a lot of ground, in particular the wild boar tenderloin, which has diners pouring in on the weekends. Cacao is a refreshing option because while most Latin American restaurants in Miami either offer steak or Cuban dishes, Cacao manages to get the best out of the continent and serves it in a modern and stylish setting. A private dining room tucked away to the side can be booked for large groups.

Food 9, Service 8, Atmosphere 7/8

Café Prima Pasta, 414 71st Street, Mid Beach
Tel: 305 867 0106
Open: midday–midnight daily $60

People in this largely Argentinian neighbourhood say they know when they have arrived home because they can smell the wafts of garlic coming from Arturo Cea's kitchen. After arriving in 1985, the Cea family, who have ancestral roots in Italy, worked as waiters and cooks in other restaurants before joining forces to create Prima Pasta in 1993. Now Papa Arturo and Mamma Carla continue to do the cooking, while Fabian takes care of the books, and Gerardo and Marcela help with menus and Café Prima Pasta's 'image'. The Ceas even offer to feed your pets while you eat either on the new, decked terrace, or in the cosy interior where the panelled walls are covered in photos of movie stars, many of whom have eaten here. The well-priced home-made pastas, seafood, veal and steaks are all fabulous, and booking is advised.

Food 8, Service 7, Atmosphere 8

Caramelo, 264 Giralda Avenue, Coral Gables
Tel: 305 445 8783
Open: midday–3pm, 6–11pm daily $90

Formerly La Bussola restaurant, a bastion of Italian dining in Coral Gables for 17 years, Caramelo continues with the Italian theme but adds a little Caribbean touch to its armoury. The restaurant's two dining rooms, bar area and cigar room are softly lit by illuminated display niches in the walls. The idea is to keep things elegant yet casual, so jackets are advised, although it's cool to have your top button undone. Meanwhile in the kitchen, co-owner Willy Fernandez is more interested in some serious pasta and meat dishes as he serves up excellent Italian fare and gar-nishes it with something sweet to give it that Caribbean touch. Booking is advised, but if you turn up without a reservation then sit on one of the comfy stools at the stylish chocolate-coloured bar and sip a cocktail until they can squeeze you in.

Food 8, Service 7, Atmosphere 7

Casa Tua, 1700 James Avenue, South Beach
Tel: 305 673 1010
Open: 11am–3pm and 6–11.30pm. Closed Sat/Sun lunch. $120

Any mention of this sleek Italian restaurant will provoke a gentle nod of approval from anyone who knows about dining in Miami. Casa Tua is a 1925 two-storey Mediterranean villa nestled away

behind hedges and an iron gate. The owner is an ex-polo patron from a wealthy family whose surfer wrist bands still poke out from the cuffs of his Armani blazer. He and his stunning hostesses happily welcome the wealthy clientele, whom they seat at a smart communal dining table or at one of the few tables in a flower and herb garden. The kitchen produces impeccably turned-out pastas and delicate Mediterranean dishes. Casa Tua will smash your Miami budget to pieces, but most people say it is worth it. Unfortunately the sleek cocktail lounge upstairs is for members only, but there is a smaller version downstairs pegged onto the restaurant.

Food 9, Service 8, Atmosphere 8

China Grill, 404 Washington Avenue, South Beach
Tel: 305 534 2211   www.chinagrillmgt.com
Open: midday–midnight (1am Fri, Sat) daily $100

This southern spin-off of Manhattan's critically acclaimed China Grill is one of South Florida's most popular dining meccas. From a distance its illuminated multicoloured tower looks more like a multistorey car park, casino and strip club than a restaurant. The

grill's clientele mixes local celebrities, the in-crowd and 'clued-in out-of-towners'. Culinarily, the menu fuses a mixture of Italian, Japanese, French, Chinese and American ingredients. Signature dishes include lobster pancakes stir-fried with red chilli, coconut milk and scallions, or tempura sashimi with hot mustard champagne sauce. Portions are very generous and can easily be shared, while the wine list is comprehensive (but expensive). If you are feeling more Japanese than Chinese, the Dragon sushi bar has been added on as a separate entity. China Grill is 'very Miami', and a restaurant that takes itself very seriously.

Food 8, Service 8, Atmosphere 7

L'Entrecôte de Paris, 419 Washington Avenue, South Beach
Tel: 305 673 1002
Open: 7pm–midnight. Closed Mondays. $80

L'Entrecôte is the closest thing to Paris on South Beach. This unpretentious little bistro can be found in one of the Beach's few tourist-free zones, but still within walking distance of the action.

Despite having both the popular Tuscan and Harrison steak houses on each side of it, L'Entrecôte's *prix fixe* menu of a salad, a choice of mussels, chicken, salmon or steak, and all the *frites* you can eat, competes well. Apart from an Argentinian steak, the menu offers exactly what you would expect from a French restaurant. Of course most of the wines on offer are French, all of the staff are French and the atmosphere is, well, very French. The clients are pretty European, too, with the odd self-professed Miami gangster popping in for a shot of cognac. L'Entrecôte is a solid choice for a date or a relaxed dinner before hitting a club.

Food 7, Service 8, Atmosphere 7

Escopazzo, 1311 Washington Avenue, South Beach
Tel: 305 674 9450 www.escopazzo.com
Open: 6pm–midnight daily $90

In 1993 owner Pino Bodini put 10 tables at the front of his family home and called it Escopazzo. Back then his mother would shout advice from the back of the kitchen while she cooked

tiramisu. Now, tiramisu remains on the pudding menu and this cosy, upscale Italian restaurant feels like the innocent little lamb of Washington Avenue, flanked by tattoo parlours and novelty shops, and filled with a loyal following of regulars and the occasional movie star to boot. In truth, Ezcopazzo is not as innocent as it looks: Pino's wife Giancarla now runs a kitchen that has become renowned for its flair. Don't expect Mamma's meatballs when eating at Ezcopazzo; Giancarla has a lot up her sleeve. Meanwhile, in Pino's cellar, there are 170 cases of wine, a fact that he openly boasts about to his patrons.

Food 9, Service 8, Atmosphere 7

The Forge, 432 Arthur Godfrey Road, South Beach
Tel: 305 538 8533 www.theforge.com
Open: 6pm–11pm (midnight Fri, Sat) daily $100

The Forge is as much of a Miami institution as it is a restaurant, a place where mobsters, presidents and movie stars used to dine shoulder-to-shoulder. Re-designed by Al Malnik in 1969 and immediately heralded as Miami's most glamorous destination, The

Forge attracted Frank Sinatra, Richard Nixon and a glittering cast of legendary figures. Inside, activity at The Forge epicentres at the bar, which separates three adjoining dining areas. The rooms are all wood-panelled with stained-glass ceilings and windows that overlook a mix of hip SoBe scenesters and wannabe gangsters who chomp firmly on cigars while their unbuttoned shirts expose some tasty gold chains. The food at The Forge is excellent, but perhaps the most impressive aspect is the wine cellar, with a list 50 pages long. Wednesday is The Forge's big night, when the rather clumsy DJ cranks things up as dinner finishes before unleashing his team of cabaret dancers. Eating here gives you automatic entrance to Jimmy'z club next door.

Food 9, Service 8, Atmosphere 9

Harrison's Steak House, 411 Washington Avenue, South Beach

Tel: 305 672 4600 www.harrisonssteakhouse.com
Open: 6.30pm–midnight daily $80

Harrison's Steak House resides in the converted Harrison's Hotel towards the end of Washington Avenue, next to La Locanda. It's Miami's answer to old-fashioned glamour; guests

move on from the solid oak bar backed with an oversized antique mirror to a formal dining arena given a stiff upper-lip by high-backed velvet velour booths, Swarovski chandeliers and a serious-looking manager. Chef Will Biscoe's menu is an offering of hefty Hereford and Kobe beef dishes and some excellent seafood for the more health conscious. The restaurant deals with a serious clientele, so while it is seldom packed, the big-spenders seem to keep things ticking over. The old school décor and carnivorous menu mean dinner at Harrison's can be a blast from South Beach's past. Harrison's also has its own lounge designed as a separate entity to the restaurant which is accessible through the front passageway, overlooked by oil paintings of topless beauties.

Food 8, Service 8, Atmosphere 7

Joe's Stone Crab, 11 Washington Avenue, South Beach
Tel: 305 673 0365   www.joesstonecrab.com
Open: 11.30am–2pm, 5–10pm (11pm Fri, Sat). Closed Sun and
Mon lunch. $75

If in doubt, South Beach locals will always point visitors in the
direction of the world-famous Joe's Stone Crab. In 1913 Joe
Weiss, the man who claimed to have discovered the edible
virtues of the stone crab, opened up Joe's Stone Crab for business and created Miami Beach's monument to informal, fine dining, a place where Al Capone, J. Edgar Hoover and the Kennedys
used to hang out. The seasonal stone crabs are served in a delicious mustard sauce, the recipe for which is apparently as secret
as the formula for Coca–Cola. For non-crab lovers there are
other dishes, but it would be a shame to ignore this restaurant's
signature dish. This is not an intimate dining location, but the
atmosphere and ultra-efficient service make for a satisfying out-
ing. They don't take reservations, so it's first come, first served,
and some will wait for hours. This is a touristy venue, but the
food is too good to ignore.

Food 9, Service 9, Atmosphere 7

La Locanda, 413 Washington Avenue, South Beach
Tel: 305 538 6277
Open: 10am–4pm (Sat/Sun) and 5.30pm–midnight daily $60

This little bambino is owned and run by an undefeated Italian boxer and an ex-Italian paratrooper, and is hands down the friendliest restaurant on South Beach. Francesco Cavalletti, who once had a promotional contract with Don King, and Massimo Fortunato, who used to jump out of aeroplanes over enemy territory, have created a charming trattoria which somehow seats 60 people. The restaurant has been squeezed in between Harrison's Steak House and French bistro L'Entrecôte, and relies on using up every inch of its allocated pavement space. The menu is not particularly adventurous, but chef Roberto Lopez and his assistant make good use of the minuscule kitchen to produce some fabulous pasta and seafood dishes that have locals coming back for more. La Locanda – which means 'inn' in Italian – is also moderately priced, so the SoBe Ferrari crowd tend to turn their noses up at it. But for those in the know who go early to grab the tables outside, La Locanda is a superb dinner venue.

Food 8, Service 8, Atmosphere 10

Mark's, Nash Hotel, 1120 Collins Avenue, South Beach
Tel: 305 604 9050. www.chefmark.com
Open: midday–3pm and 7–11pm daily $70

Mark's at the Nash Hotel is owned by and named after Mark Militello, who was once ranked among the 'Ten best chefs in

America'. The restaurateur runs four kitchens in South Florida and continues to win accolades in high-profile publications for his skills in an apron. He leaves Larry La Valley to run the kitchen in his absence, and Larry does an excellent job, creating most of the menu himself. Larry caters for almost all tastes, changing the menu almost every day, so even the pickiest of diners should find something they like here. The restaurant is on the verge of being stylish as it boasts a sleek wooden counter, which is visible from the Nash Hotel's lobby. But the verdict is still out as to whether Mark's will become part of the furniture on South Beach.

Food 8, Service 8, Atmosphere 6

Metro Kitchen, Astor Hotel, 956 Washington Avenue, South Beach

Tel: 305 672 7217   www.metrokitchenbar.com
Open: 7.30–11.30 am and 7pm (midday Sat/Sun)–midnight (1am Fri/Sat) daily $90

Booking a table at Metro Kitchen in the Astor Hotel automatically guarantees entrance to the Metro Bar, a venue so popular on a Tuesday evening that people regularly attempt to climb over a 10-foot wall at the neighbouring Chelsea Hotel to gain entry. Both restaurant and bar are co-owned by Mynt's Nicola Siervo. Mynt is probably the hippest nightclub on South Beach (see

Party), so it follows that her restaurant and bar would kick up the same amount of fuss. Realistically, Metro Kitchen would not be so popular if it were being judged solely on its food. In fact, people who go to Metro Kitchen don't seem to be that interested in the cuisine. The food is tasty and impeccably presented, but doesn't quite warrant the high prices. Chefs Michael Rodriguez and Mike Neal offer some promising eclectic American dishes, but their assistants do not deliver when the going gets tough on a busy evening. For best results at Metro Kitchen, book a table on any night other than Tuesday – the standard of food improves dramatically.

Food 6, Service 7, Atmosphere 9

Nemo, 100 Collins Avenue, South Beach
Tel: 305 532 4550
Open: midday (11am Sun)–3pm and 7pm–midnight daily $85

The clever thing about Nemo is that you can't decide whether you are sitting inside or out, thanks to its cheeky outdoorsy design. The arches and airy interior somehow set the senses free, creating a feeling of laid-back sophistication. The inside is divided up into a copper bar area and a dining room consisting of round tables lit by lamps that whirl down from the ceiling on copper wiring that matches the bar top. The menu offers a satisfying range of dishes, with the pick of the bunch probably being the sea bass. Portions are not huge, so keep Hedy Goldsmith, the renowned pastry chef, on her toes by ordering something chocolatey and indulgent. The mood is friendly and the service professional and unpretentious. Nemo is also blessed by having the Room Bar, a small dark cavern-like alehouse and winery, which most people try to keep a secret, just yards away around the corner.

Food 8, Service 8, Atmosphere 9

Nobu, The Shore Club, 1901 Collins Avenue, South Beach
Tel: 305 695 3100
Open: 7pm–1am daily $90

Book well in advance to score a table at Nobuyuki Matsuhisa's Miami Beach branch of his 12-restaurant Nobu empire. The restaurant is hidden at the back of The Shore Club hotel beside Robert de Niro's Italian investment Ago. Chef Thomas Buckley takes the reigns having honed his skills at Nobu London before landing on Miami Beach. Apparently he paid particular attention when learning about rock shrimp tempura: this signature dish is a work of art, as is the much-copied black cod with miso. If your concierge fails to land a table for you, the alternative is to turn up and hope there is room at the bar area, where ultra-toned bartenders look after rowdy businessmen who like to flash their cash, and cosmopolitan-drinking blondes wait to pick up their sugar daddies. After dinner, roll on to Sky Bar, which is also at The Shore Club.

Food 9/10, Service 8, Atmosphere 9

Norman's, 21 Almeria Avenue, Coral Gables
Tel: 305 446 6767 www.normans.com
Open: 6–10pm (10.30pm Fri, Sat). Closed Sundays. $100

Norman's is perhaps the most famous of all the restaurants in Coral Gables. Named after Frenchman Norman Van Aken, the

restaurant has won countless awards since opening in 1995. The building looks pretty scrubby on the outside, perched on the corner of a rather suburban area, but the interior is decorated in the smooth Spanish-colonial style that the district is known for. The setting is all very relaxed, but smart–casual attire is recommended. Norman is one of the chefs that put South Florida on the culinary map, so his New World cuisine, or fusion of native and island ingredients with a thorough knowledge of French cooking techniques, is worth booking a table for. Because Norman's is so well known for its food, all sorts of people go there to eat and the atmosphere is always friendly. If you are serious about your food, then this is a good place to start.

Food 9, Service 8, Atmosphere 7/8

Ola, 5061 Biscayne Boulevard, Downtown
Tel: 305 758 9195
Open: 5pm–midnight daily $70

Ola sits among the up-and-coming stretch of restaurants on Biscayne Boulevard and has a very sleek, modern design, with space-age chairs, abstract art and a long retro table as the centre-piece. Chef Douglas Rodriguez first opened Yuca in Coral Gables, and Ola is his latest venture, producing a serious mixture of Latin American recipes that most chefs in Miami would never consider. Ceviches, however, are what Douglas is renowned for;

in fact, he has written a book called *The Great Ceviche*. With less competition in the area, Ola is fast becoming popular and is therefore an ideal place to eat if you plan to hit clubs in the Downtown area. The atmosphere is usually friendly as people arrive either directly from work or turn up later for dinner before heading to Pawn Shop and I/O (see Party).

Food 8, Service 7, Atmosphere 8

One Ninety, Albion Hotel, 1650 James Avenue, Miami Beach
Tel: 305 913 1000
Open: 6pm–midnight. Closed Mondays. $60

Do not be alarmed if you find Argentinian chef Alan Hughes lying down when you walk into One Ninety. Alan often likes to cook quickly and rest with his guests as they eat his food on deep,

comfy sofas that sit under the palm trees of the Albion Hotel's courtyard. After relocating One Ninety from the Design District to the Albion's courtyard, Alan now quietly flashes his pans on a grill so basic that it resembles an industrial Sunday afternoon barbecue. The last thing you would expect is culinary genius. But Alan makes a mockery of all modern kitchens in Miami as he carefully churns out exquisite dishes. The simplicity of the cooking, the chilled setting, the DJ spinning in the background, all combine to create one of South Beach's finest eating arenas. The food here is also surprisingly cheap for Miami standards – given the cooking facilities, it's probably helped by the low electricity bill.

Food 9/10, Service 9, Atmosphere 9

Ortanique on the Mile, 278 Miracle Mile, Coral Gables
Tel: 305 446 7710 www.cindyhutsoncuisine.com
Open: 11.30am–2.30pm, 6–10pm (11pm Thurs–Sat, 9.30pm Sun).
Closed lunchtimes Sat/Sun. $85

Chef and co-owner Cindy Hutson used to skipper a 36-foot fishing boat on which she would prepare and cook the fish for her passengers. She then brought her seafaring knowledge back to dry land to start a South Beach restaurant before opening Ortanique in the Coral Gables restaurant arena. In addition to her knowledge of fish, she also brought back a bizarre love for Caribbean oranges. The curtains, doors, plates, menus, pillars and tables at the restaurant are all decorated with orange motifs as she and her partner Delius Shirley remind us that the 'ortanique'

is actually an orange native to Jamaica. The décor is a little sickly, but Ortanique on the Mile serves some excellent signature dishes such as mussels in spicy Jamaican Red-Stripe beer and a West Indian style bouillabaisse. Chefs in the area always recommend this restaurant and it is regularly packed, so booking is advisable.

Food 9, Service 8, Atmosphere 7

Osteria del Teatro, 1443 Washington Avenue, South Beach
Tel: 305 538 7850
Open: 6–11pm. Closed Sundays. $60

The restaurant sits beside a former theatre that has now become the Crobar nightclub, one of the centres of decadence on Miami Beach (see Party). This is not an especially trendy venue, but the specials board at Osteria del Teatro is so good that its tiny dining area brims with tourists and locals every evening from six o'clock onwards. Take no notice of the pink menus here; instead listen to the waiter proudly reel off a long list of goodies. The design is a simple combination of white table-cloths and bright walls topped off with some fiery modern paint-ings. The floor-to-ceiling windows, however, give a far more inter-esting view of Miami Beach's eclectic band of party-goers on their way to drink themselves senseless at Crobar. Dinner at Osteria is excellent, but be careful not to lick your lips too much or you may have kisses blown at you by the transvestites on their way next door.

Food 8, Service 9, Atmosphere 7

Pacific Time, 915 Lincoln Road, South Beach
Tel: 305 534 5979 www.pacifictime.biz
Open: 11.45am–2.30pm, 6–11pm (midnight Fri, Sat) daily $100

Pacific Time is easily the best eatery on Lincoln Road, so if you're
looking to dine well in the heart of the South Beach action, this
is an excellent choice. The restaurant was founded in 1993 when
Jonathan Eismann left a prospering career in New York's restaurant scene and pumped his hard-earned cash into creating Pacific
Time. The move turned out to be a good one as his restaurant
leads the field in terms of innovative cooking. Now dozens of
awards hang on the warehouse-like walls, which have been plas-
tered over in random patches to create that storm-stricken
Pacific island hut feel. The exterior looks like any other on
Lincoln Road, but the food is in a class of its own, offering a really good selection of Pan-Asian fish and crab dishes. The restaurant accommodates about a hundred, but there is seating outside
where you can watch the people walk or skate by in the best
rags on Lincoln Road.

Food 9/10, Service 8, Atmosphere 7

Prime One Twelve, 112 Ocean Drive, Miami Beach
Tel: 305 532 8112
Open: midday–3pm, 6.30pm–midnight daily $100

If you're vegetarian, do not approach the bar (or the dining room
for that matter) – apparently peanuts went out of style years ago
and bacon is back in fashion. It's probably best to retreat past
the hopefuls outside leaning on Lamborghini bonnets and waiting
for a table. This is the 'in' place to eat on Miami Beach, so even if
you do book a table you will be sent to the exceptionally stylish

but crowded bar. The main dining area is on the ground floor, but
there are a couple of more intimate dining rooms on the first
floor of the old Brown's Hotel. Prime One Twelve is a steak
house. It does offer some delicate alternatives, but it would be a
shame not to indulge in the rather expensive yet tender steaks
served here. Like any hip restaurant in Miami, be prepared to
wait for your table, for the waiters to give you attitude and for
the food and wine to be overpriced.

Food 8, Service 5, Atmosphere 7

Romeo's Café, 2257 Coral Way, Coral Gables
Tel: 305 859 2228
Open: midday–3pm (Tues–Fri) and 6–11pm (midnight Fri/Sat,
10pm Sun) daily $85

There are no menus at this dark little dining room, which is lit
only by a fish tank and a couple of candles. What you eat here
rather depends on how your chat goes with Romeo Marjano,
the owner and chef, who scuttles around the tiny 26-cover

dining room gauging what everybody likes and dislikes. For $65 a head, he'll tailor his northern Italian-influenced dishes to your tastes. Officially he'll cook you six courses of whatever you want, but in reality Romeo cooks the same dish for everybody with a few variations. With Romeo in Italian mode, the courses are small, making it possible to conquer the full six. If you dislike something, then the efficient waiters will bring you another dish as soon as Romeo has decided on a suitable substitute. The darkness does hide a pretty sketchy wine list, however. To find the restaurant look out for the dark green awnings.

Food 9, Service 8, Atmosphere 8

Shoji Sushi, 100 Collins Avenue, South Beach
Tel: 305 532 4245 www.sojisushi.com
Open: midday–3pm, 6pm–1am daily $60

Shoji Sushi is a relaxing spot to nibble on some of the best sushi in town and sip at a vat of cold sake. Opened in 2001, the restaurant is connected to both sister restaurant Nemo and the Mercury Hotel located at the southern end of Collins Avenue. If the weather is good, which it usually is in Miami, then it is worth sitting outside under the palm trees. Otherwise head inside to watch master sushi chef Shingo 'Shin' Inoue, who used to work at Nobu in Malibu, prepare exquisite sushi rolls. The service is impeccable at Shoji Sushi, and the waiters will never allow your glass to be empty. The food is also reasonably priced here, so a mixture of up-and-coming fashion photographers, models who pay for themselves and the usual South Beach big-shots show up. There is usually no need to book a table, and even if the restaurant is full, there is usually not too much of a wait.

Food 9, Service 10, Atmosphere 8

Smith & Wollensky, 1 Washington Avenue (at South Pointe Park), South Beach
Tel: 305 673 2800 www.smithandwollensky.com
Open: midday–2am Mon–Sat; 11.30am–2am Sun $85

The Miami branch sits right on the waterfront at the tip of South Beach, with views of the Atlantic Ocean and the Downtown

skyline. It's a superb location for dinner or brunch. Assume all the American culinary classics to be on offer as well as some exciting salads on chef Robert Mignola's menu, and expect a packed house inside the two-storey building. Surprisingly this is one of the only restaurants on South Beach that overlooks the Ocean, so it is advisable to book a table outside where the tables almost touch the grass at the waterfront, and there is a nice long bar where guests have the most fun. The view crosses Miami's main shipping channel, so yachts, big vulgar speedboats and gigantic cruise ships pass by as you sip your Manhattan. The bottom line is that Smith & Wollensky is one of the best steak houses in town, and it has the best view of them all.

Food 8, Service 8, Atmosphere 8

Spiga, 1228 Collins Avenue, South Beach
Tel: 305 534 0079
Open: 6–11pm (midnight Fri, Sat) daily $70

Spiga (Italian for wheat), has been on South Beach for almost a decade, which in Miami terms means the food has continued to attract the customers long after the restaurant became old news. Managed by owner Roberto Legrand, Spiga seats around 50 and welcomes anyone through the doors. The clean lines, white tablecloths and wooden bar make this is a very welcoming Italian. It is not quite in the same league as Escopazzo or Casa Tua because the menu is not as adventurous and, well, Spiga is not as ambitious as its Italian counterparts. But with a constantly

changing and properly priced specials board as well as the staple pasta, risotto and fish dishes, Spiga is a coolly underestimated dining venue. Generally this is a popular spot for a date or a relaxing dinner, but this is a very down-to-earth restaurant where staff are always keen on cranking things up.

Food 8, Service 8, Atmosphere 7

Sushi Samba Dromo, 600 Lincoln Road, South Beach
Tel: 305 673 5337 www.sushisamba.com
Open: midday–midnight (2am Fri, Sat) daily $75

On hearing an elderly client ask why Sushi Samba was always being mentioned in papers alongside the name of a big French hotel called Paris Hilton, a waiter at Sushi Samba was so offended he threatened to spike her sake for blasphemy – or so the story goes. Sushi Samba is known as much for its celebrity sightings as for its blend of Japanese, Brazilian and Peruvian cuisine.

The truth about Sushi Samba is that the food is average to good, the interior's bubbly ceiling transforms the space into what looks like a set on an Austin Powers film, the waiters pout just as much as the customers, and the people who eat there want to be seen. All in all, it is worth making the trip down trendy Lincoln Road just to sit outside at Sushi Samba, sip on warm sake and munch on a big portion of dragon rolls.

Food 7, Service 7, Atmosphere 9

Taverna Opa, 36 Ocean Drive, South Beach
Tel: 305 673 6730 www.tavernaoparestaurant.com
Open: 4pm until the ouzo runs out (about 4am) daily $70

Taverna Opa is the South Beach Greek fest where locals go to give their Miami beach poker faces a night off and let their hair down for some ouzo-fuelled crockery-smashing with some table-dancing therapy. It's an ideal place to take a group of friends out for a booze-fuelled thriller. The menu is all about lamb: lamb shank, fire-roasted lamb and lamb chops are all available, while there is also an assortment of grilled seafood for those sick of lamb. The Greek flags and paintings create that Miami authentic

Greek party feeling, while the tables are dressed to a minimum, allowing easy access to the table-tops for when the music is turned up. Women are advised not to wear high heels.

Food 7, Service 8, Atmosphere 9

Touch, 910 Lincoln Road, South Beach
Tel: 305 532 8003 www.touchrestaurant.com
Open: 7pm–midnight (1am Fri, Sat) daily $85

On entering Touch, guests will be greeted by two hostesses on a

velvet-covered swing. The softly lit interior is one big open space with a round bar and two levels of seating. With the lampshades stuck to the wall, it looks rather like a mini version of the lobby at the Ritz Carlton. The idea is that the higher you are placed, the more important you feel. From the kitchen chef Sean Brasel says he just loves to cook with foie gras, lobster, oysters and caviar, which is probably how he justifies the high prices, and the truth is that these are ingredients that people in Miami are most impressed by. It all sounds luxurious and in the end it tastes very

good. After dinner the belly-dancers will appear, live music is played, and what was a cushioned dining den becomes a full-on party zone.

Food 7, Service 8, Atmosphere 8

Tuscan Steak, 431 Washington Avenue, South Beach
Tel: 305 534 2233 www.chinagrillmanagement.com
Open: 6–11pm (midnight Fri, Sat) daily $80

If there were a ranking for biggest plate of food, then Tuscan Steak would rate very highly for its Flinstonian-sized T-bones, side dishes and inventive salads that are all meant to be shared. This family-style Florentine steak house has the same owners as China Grill (which is just across the road), so a high standard of service and food are pretty much guaranteed. The interior's rough stone walls, dark wood floors and wooden furniture are gently illuminated with soft lighting and white tablecloths (rare in Miami), creating a cosy atmosphere. If stiff drinks are on your checklist, then there is plenty of room at Tuscan's 44-foot long granite bar which runs the length of the dining area and serves some sizeable cocktails.

Food 8, Service 8, Atmosphere 7

Wish, The Hotel, 801 Collins Avenue, South Beach
Tel: 305 674 9474
Open: 11.30am–3pm, 6–11pm (midnight Fri, Sat) $85

Located on the premises of The Hotel, Wish's cosy garden dining area is accessible from the hotel veranda or from the street.

Chef Michael Bloise, who used to work at Miami's Tantra restaurant, and fashion designer cum décor specialist Todd Oldham (who decorated The Hotel's interior) have made this into an excellent option for a quiet dinner date. Oldham's oasis-style al fresco eating arena under palm trees and satellite dish umbrellas feels tucked away and secluded, while Bloise's perfectly cooked seafood dishes will appear in front of you within minutes. After dinner it would be a shame to miss out on Wish's speciality cocktails, which are lit up by floating neon ice cubes. This is very Miami, and extremely tacky, but head up to the roof pool area for some shameless lounging.

Food 9, Service 10, Atmosphere 7

drink...

Drinking in Miami is more problematic than you might think. The city is known for its dinner and dancing, but the bit in between is not as clear-cut as one would expect in the party capital of Florida.

For a start, there is a well-established trend of hanging out in hotel lobby bars – the idea being that if you can't stay there, you might as well be seen drinking there. (See 'For Hotel Lobby Junkies', on page 92, for where to go and when.)

As well as cocktail-sipping in a hotel lobby or poolside, however, it is becoming fashionable to get gritty and go to scrubby dive bars, as it was a couple of years ago in New York, which means, luckily, in certain places it is now cool to be uncool. Good news then for all of us, including the author, as this means there are now bars in Miami where you can order a beer without being looked at by the locals as if you are about to drink a pint of poison. Miami's top dive bar is Club Deuce on 14th Street, although this could prove to be a little too much of a dive bar initiation for some.

For a something a little more low-key and funky, head to the secret Room Bar, which is a little hide-out almost at the tip of South Beach. If live music's your

choice look no further than Jazid on Washington Avenue, which always has talented (and sometimes not quite so talented) musicians playing in its small downstairs bar area.

For no-holes-barred places to get hammered, Automatic Slims and Purdy Lounge top the range, ASBO awarding cocktails, slammers and shooters are the order of the day. Both these are high-octane, testosterone-fuelled binge-drinking destinations, where total oblivion is all but guaranteed.

Stepping up into the slightly underground but very trendy section, there's Buck 15 – a converted loft space filled with old sofas found in flea markets, but with a really hip atmosphere. Along with Rok Bar, this is Miami's top bar for undeniable trendiness.

Moving on and more upscale is Sky Bar, which technically qualifies as a hotel lobby bar. Nevertheless, Sky Bar is a bar and it always attracts a fashionable group of locals and spruced-up tourists. But Rok Bar is two steps up from any other on the Miami scene, and is packed every night of the week.

In terms of the best-looking bartenders, the Coyote Ugly-style girls at Automatic Slims who pour shots down people's throats are interesting to watch, while it is always a pleasure to wait to be served at Rok Bar.

And lastly, an insider's tip to help you on your way – drinking beer in most fashionable places is frowned upon, in part because it's the cheapest thing on the menu, but mainly because it's so 'unsophisticated'. If you have to order an ale and want to look the part, ask the bartender for an imported lager such as Heineken. If it's foreign, it's game. It sounds ridiculous, but this *is* Miami.

FOR HOTEL LOBBY JUNKIES

Monday: The Delano Hotel's Rose Bar and its pool area have traditionally been top places to be seen, but in recent times the Delano has become a little passé. However, Monday nights are still popular and will continue for a while yet.

Tuesday: The Hotel Astor's Metro Bar is now ingrained on the social calendar of the Miami lobby junkie. The Metro Bar is only really hot on a Tuesday evening, so doesn't qualify as a bar in itself, but the Tuesday night Metro session will open your eyes to what Miami is all about.

Wednesday: It's a risky call giving Circa 39 the Wednesday night spot, given that Wednesday is such a pivotal day in the Miami week and Circa 39 is so new. But this lobby bar is up-and-coming. Circa 39 is out of the way, 'mid beach', but there is a cheeky crowd who have decided to make it their naughty little secret spot. If the Circa 39 movement peters out try the Sky Bar, or just head to Buck 15.

Thursday: The Spire Bar at The Hotel is becoming a bit of a dark horse, hardly publicized but seriously cool, like The Townhouse's Deck Bar. The Hotel allows both guests and outsiders to enjoy the rooftop rather than closing it off and reserving it for the penthouse suite.

Friday: It takes a tough bar to outscore The Hotel's Spire Bar, but the lighting is better on The Townhouse's rooftop deck. The deck itself has a slightly warmer feel to it, and the sun beds are water beds, which nobody can deny that they love. If you find yourself in Downtown early evening, head to the Mandarin Oriental's beach party to kick back and start the weekend with a Martini and a preppy crowd.

Saturday: Sky Bar at the Shore Club is so much more than a lobby bar. It's a full-on bar that's almost a nightclub. At the time of writing, the Setai hotel was building its answer to the lobby bar and restaurant, which will surely be a hotspot on a Saturday evening.

Sunday: The week is wrapped up fittingly by Raleigh Hotel, which makes a play for the top spot. The Raleigh's pool party on a Sunday afternoon is the holy grail of Miami drinking arenas. Go there to see why. At night the Raleigh's garden is as chilled a spot as you will find on the Beach.

On the eighth day: No Miami lobby bar appraisal would be complete without mentioning the Whitelaw Hotel's bar. The really savvy local knows that this is a bargain hotel with a killer, white leather bar. It's good everyday and every afternoon and is ideally positioned for some people watching.

The Abbey, 1115 16th Street, South Beach
Tel: 305 538 8110
Open: 1pm–5am daily

The Abbey is hard to find (look out for the tiny sign above the door), and inside it's rather like an English pub – a wooden affair, with wooden bar stools and a row of tables overlooked by an

abstract Madonna painting – but it has the soul of a dive bar. In fact The Abbey bills itself as the oldest bar on Miami Beach, a claim that would anger the crowd down at Club Deuce if they were sober enough to take it in. Locals love to drink here when they are fed up with South Beach, or when they just want a bit of innocent chitchat, so artificiality and pretension are left at the door, behind which the dartboard is located. The Abbey offers five of its own brews, including a stout, as well as serving commercial beers. Do not, whatever you do, order a mojito.

Automatic Slims, 1216 Washington Avenue, South Beach
Tel: 305 695 0795
Open: 8pm (4pm Fri–Sun)–5am daily

Automatic Slims is the bar where the beautiful go to get ugly. It's now a bit of a cliché to describe somewhere as a 'Coyote Ugly' bar – where people get as drunk as possible, and the pretty bar girls dance on the bar or around a stripper's pole before pouring liquor down people's throats – but this is exactly the case. This is a rock'n'roll bar that gets packed with a young, fun crowd, many of whom are beautiful enough to get into Mansion nightclub on the other side of the road, but who prefer to hear Guns'n'Roses and slam Tequila shots at the bar. There is no cover charge and the drinks are reasonably priced for Miami. On Wednesdays local bands are invited to play and on Thursdays it's Ladies' Night when the girls drink for free after 10pm.

Bahia, Four Seasons, 1435 Brickell Avenue, Downtown
Tel: 305 358 3535 www.fourseasons.com
Open: 5–11pm (midnight Thurs–Sat) daily

Bahia takes the hotel bar culture very seriously. Located beside the hotel's pool area, this is a city slickers' bar with attitude, where yuppies and career girls make their way from work and other pretty women go to be met. You can choose from high chairs along an impeccably kept stainless-steel bar or wicker chairs at wooden tables, and there's a snazzy waterfall feature as a backdrop. Where to mingle? Take your pick, but most people hover somewhere between the two and peer towards Biscayne Bay, which separates the financial district and South Beach. Drinks are priced on the Upper East Side but luckily there is a bank in the building. If you are in Miami on business, then Bahia is a suitable place to forget or prepare for a meeting, depending on your work ethic.

Blue, 222 Espanola Way, South Beach
Tel: 305 534 1009
Open: 10pm–5am daily

Shaped like a teardrop and lit up in blue, Blue is a futuristic-style bar ideal for a first or second stop on a big night out. Centrally located on South Beach beside sister pool bar Lost Weekend on Espanola Way, Blue is 50 yards from Crobar nightclub on the corner of Washington Avenue (see Party). The bar begins to fill after 10pm, but peaks after midnight when things can get a little silly – which is precisely why Blue is to be seen only as a useful bit-part to a big night out. It's affordable and slightly rough around the edges, and it stays open until 5am, which means a young and friendly crowd turns up. Technically it's a nightclub, but treat Blue as a bar, enjoy your generously poured and well-priced cocktail, and head out to the next venue.

Buck 15, 707 Lincoln Lane, South Beach
Tel: 305 538 3815 www.buck15.com
Open: 10pm (8pm Fri/Sat)–5am. Closed Sundays and Mondays.

Buck 15 is an overground underground bar dressed in a funky 1970s industrial outfit. The space was converted by Jennie Yip who owns the popular Chinese restaurant Miss Yip Café below. The entrance is around the back of the restaurant and the bar can be reached via a stairway covered in graffiti art. The bar area is a sitting room filled with 1970s sofas picked up in flea markets

and is decorated in street art canvases and skateboards (stuck on the wall) designed by local artists. Individually this upholstery could make you feel nauseous, but collectively the sofas and artwork blend to create Miami's top retro lounge. The bar supports local emerging artists, musicians and designers, so the crowd is relaxed. But the originality of the place is fast making it into the coolest underground place to hang out in Miami. Proceedings are casually overlooked by a giant sumo wrestler painted onto the back wall. Have a look at the shops on Lincoln Road, pop round the corner to eat at Miss Yip's and drink a few beers in a choice velvet sofa or special Buck 15 love seat.

Club Deuce, 222 14th Street, South Beach
Tel: 305 531 6200
Open: 8am–5am daily

Some Miami locals boast that they don't go out on a Saturday night but instead get up at the crack of dawn on a Sunday and go to the Deuce for the SoBe after-party at 8am. The Deuce, as they fondly call it, is the authentic Miami dive of old – a relic of the day when cocaine and gunshot wounds were as common as sunburn on South Beach – and it is proud to admit it. The bar is not pretty, nor is the bartender; but that is its charm. All sorts of people drink at the Deuce. It's a place where strippers and glamour models play each other at pool for their next shot of whisky. So if you don't like the high-hooch club scene at Miami,

put the olive back in your Martini, head towards the Deuce, order a beer and sit safe in the knowledge that you might end up talking to a transvestite, a Hollywood actor, or a lorry driver from Texas. The possibilities are endless.

Finnegan's Way, 1344 Ocean Drive, South Beach
Tel: 305 672 7747 www.finnegansway.com
Open: 9am–4am daily

If you want to drink a pint of beer without people thinking you are a heathen, or if the mojitos are just getting too much for you, Finnegan's Way offers the Irish alternative to Ocean Drive. To really soak up Ocean Drive it is best to start the tour at the southern end and work your way up through the crowds. Finnegan's is located at the northern end of the road, away from most of the tourists, so it can be a welcome resting-post. There is a bar inside, but the outdoor bar is where the action happens. Finnegan's fills up in the late afternoon and early evening and is a prime spot for watching sports.

Flute Champagne Bar, 500 South Point Drive, South Beach
Tel: 305 748 8680 www.flutebar.com
Open: 8pm (5pm Fri)–5am daily

Sister champagne bar to Flute in New York's Flatiron building, Flute is a magnet for men who adore to be seen spending money in an 'exclusive' setting. Champagne, as the bar's name suggests, is the drink of choice, with non-vintage and vintage bottles on offer. To look the part at Flute, go and see the manager before it gets busy and tell him to greet you with open arms and

remember your name on your arrival later. That way the girls in your entourage will be impressed. Seriously, this is Miami, and there are actually men who do this. Flute has cosy private alcoves set around a horseshoe-shaped bar dwarfed by racks of champagne and a crystal chandelier hung from a double-height ceiling. To really get a taste of Miami, pop into Flute at the southern end of South Beach after midnight for a champagne cocktail; or perhaps blend in a little further, book an alcove and lie back in a cushioned mini-lounge behind your own private velvet rope. Bottles cost from $50 to $500, which is surprisingly cheap by Miami standards.

Gordon Biersch Brewery, 1201 Brickell Avenue, Miami
Tel: 786 452 1130 www.gordonbiersch.com
Open: 11.30am–midnight

Gordon Biersch Brewery is located on Brickell Avenue in Miami's financial district, a block away from the Conrad Hotel and the Four Seasons. The bar fills up with businessmen ready to let off

steam after work and is a fiery venue to exchange business cards. This is predominantly a restaurant, but there are bar stools and mingling space that will accommodate at least 100 people. This is not a bar for an evening drink, but it is a useful pit-stop for after the office.

Harrison's, Harrison's Steakhouse, 411 Washington Avenue, South Beach

Tel: 305 672 4600 www.harrisonssteakhouse.com
Open: 10pm–4am daily

If you are going to dinner at Harrison's Steakhouse, La Locanda, L'Entrecôte or Tuscan Steak then look no further than Harrison's lounge bar behind the restaurant if you fancy going for a drink as

well. Long leather sofas work as the centrepiece to this old hall illuminated by colour-changing light panels. The wood flooring and solid oak bar create a classic Art Deco ambience of old. The lounge occasionally gets busy on weekends, but can be good just for a few relaxing drinks after dinner.

Jazid, 1342 Washington Avenue, South Beach
Tel: 305 673 9372 www.jazid.net
Open: 9pm–5am daily

Do not expect to hear jazz when entering Jazid, unless you can hear the Dizzy Gillespie in the live reggae, rock, R&B and Latin fusion performed nightly. Originally the idea was to entice South

Beach's nocturnal warriors with a spot of jazz. But South Beach is not the kind of place where you sit down and savour the sounds of trumpets, saxophones and pianos. On South Beach the idea is to get drunk, look cool and get dancing (if that's possible), so now Jazid packs people into its cramped interior and feeds them beer, vodka and live music. Upstairs there's a DJ lounge with a pool table and cocktail bar, but the main events happen downstairs where performances start at 9pm. People dress casually at Jazid, so tanktops and jeans are acceptable. There is a cover charge of $10, but if you look confident at the door then the doorman should let you off paying. The acoustic rock session on a Monday can be interesting.

M-Bar, Mandarin Oriental, 500 Brickell Key Drive, Miami
Tel: 305 913 8383 www.mandarinoriental.com
Open: 5pm–midnight (1am Sat/Sun)

M-Bar at the Mandarin Oriental hotel offers over 250 varieties of Martini, the largest selection in South Florida. The bar itself is topped with Blue Bahia, which we are informed is the finest, most expensive marble on the planet. Not quite as expensive, but easily more impressive are floor-to-ceiling windows that

expose panoramic views of Biscayne Bay and the Miami skyline. M-Bar attracts Miami's business in-crowd, those who love their suits and those who like to dress up after a hard day at the beach and pretend they have been chained to a desk all day. The party on Friday evenings has become a well-known event in the Miami party schedule. M-Bar opens at 5pm and serves sushi nibbles for those stopping off on the way back from work.

Monty's, 303 Alton Road, South Beach
Tel: 305 673 3444 www.montysstonecrab.com
Open: 11am–midnight (2am Fri/Sat) daily

Monty's is the only bar that overlooks the South Beach marina. The building looks like a tacky burger joint when approached by road, but the pool-side bar area furthest from the restaurant must be judged on its own merit. The bar sits below a thatched palm roof and is only yards away from the lines of budget powerboats that serve as its backdrop. Don't be tempted to swim in the pool, as all sorts of things, including cocktails and intoxicated birthday boys, are thrown in after dark. Monty's attracts the kind of weekend drinker that likes to start early, so happy hour on a Friday evening is the best time to see Monty's in full flow. It also attracts the weekday early drinker for that matter, starting its four-hour happy hour session at 4pm daily. Oysters, clams and shrimp are also available at the bar. This is also a suitable place for a drink after a scuba-diving or fishing trip.

Purdy Lounge, 1811 Purdy Avenue, South Beach
Tel: 305 531 4622 www.purdylounge.com
Open: 3pm (6pm Sat/Sun)–5am daily

It's worth getting in a taxi just to watch the surfing videos projected onto big screens at Purdy Lounge. Lit by low-slung aluminium lamps hanging from the ceiling and lava lamps on the walls, the bar has a bohemian vibe to it. Purdy Lounge is always busy and the atmosphere is like that of an upscale frat-house party. There are a few tables where you can sit either on giant hand chairs or sofas, but Purdy Lounge is all about standing up and drinking in a crowded but laid-back room. Like most serious entertainment establishments in Miami, the bar stays open until 5am. Thursday is Ladies' Night when girls drink for free, and the men follow, and on a Sunday they host a chocolate party in an attempt to keep the weekend party going.

Rok Bar, 1905 Collins Avenue, South Beach
Tel: 305 538 7171 www.rokbarmiami.com
Open: 9pm–4am daily

If in doubt, always go to Rok Bar – which is so much more than just a bar. It's like a retro mini Studio 54 with funky red lights on the ceiling and giant rock-chic hero figures lit up behind the bar. Many of Miami's most beautiful girls come to party here, but the tall pair of blonde bartenders dressed in tiny shredded outfits are the most popular figures in the house. They serve the drinks

with some serious attitude and will ignore punters all night unless tipped well. The DJ is well educated in all rock genres and gets people dancing as the night progresses. Tables can be booked here, but the small lounge area towards the entrance is only really used by people who are about to pass out. Entrance is free, but an early arrival is paramount because this place fills up quickly after midnight with the hippest of Miami crowds. Like Mynt next door (see Party), the more girls you arrive with, the more likely it is that manager Ethen Asch will let you in.

The Room, 100 Collins Avenue, Suite 4 (entrance on 1st Street between Collins and Washington Avenue), South Beach
Tel: 305 531 6061
Open: 6pm–2am daily

Locals like to keep this tiny little bar a secret from tourists, although the specials board says the bar is still available for photo shoots. It is not often that you find a secret location in Miami, but it is a pleasure when this does happen. The Room is a recent addition to South Beach that serves an international selection of beer and wine, and has no intention of introducing a cocktail shaker to its toolbox. Brown padded sofa stools hug a curved bar lit up by dimmed spotlights and candles, while there are other high tables and additional sofas at the back. The Room is small and attracts a loyal following of locals from 6pm

onwards when hairdressers, businessmen and photographers sip on continental lager and Yorkshire brown ale. Later on The Room brims with additional waitresses and clientele from the restaurants around the corner until the room runs out. This is the perfect bar for a drink before or after dining at Nemo, Prime One Twelve and Shoji Sushi just yards away around the corner. It is also close to Nikki Beach, Pearl, Opium Garden and Privé nightclubs. Photographers should bring additional lighting when shooting here.

Rose Bar, Delano Hotel, 1685 Collins Avenue, South Beach
Tel: 305 674 6400 www.delanohotelmiami.com
Open: midday–midnight (1am Fri/Sat) daily

Miami's top social radar scanners will tell you that the Delano Hotel is slightly passé. However, this is a hotel that has kicked up a fuss around the world, so a trip to the Rose Bar is an enjoyable way to see exactly why. Rose Bar is a stylish sidekick to the Delano's towering lobby, and is cleverly lit by red tinted spotlights, blending in well with the lobby's dark tanned walls and wooden floor. This is an inviting place to sit on cushioned stools or play a frame of pool, if the models will let you play. The coin on the table technique does not seem to work with them. But sometimes it's just best to sit back and let them show you how the game should be played. Rose Bar still attracts an interesting

crowd as this is a really stylish bar in an impressive setting. Ignore anyone who says otherwise. The cocktails are as strong and expensive as ever.

Royal Bar, 761 Washington Avenue, South Beach
Tel: 305 300 0221
Open: 24 hours daily

The owner of Royal Bar will look you up and down on his television screen before permitting you access to his underground after-parties, which begin at 4am. The entrance is behind the building, on Pennsylvania Avenue. If you arrive before midnight then go to the front entrance on Washington Avenue where there are no cameras, just a bouncer who could ask you whether you are there to compete in the rap-off battle in the Wednesday Respect session hosted by the resident DJ. Royal Bar is a long and thin den decked out with sofas with a stage at the middle point between the bar and a lounge. The music is either hip-hop or rap, depending on the resident DJ of the night. It's a

suitable venue for early morning/after party drinking and is regularly frequented by a fun crowd of hip-hop fans (and sometimes a hysterical Anglo-American who thinks he owns the place).

Safari Bar at the Chesterfield Hotel consumes the hotel's lobby and terrace, which overlooks the really interesting part of Collins Avenue. Either relax on the terrace's large dark sofas and let yourself be entertained by the men driving past as slowly as possible to show off their spoilers, or by the women that strut past having just spent somebody's hard-earned cash in the boutique stores near by. This is a perfect spot to rest tired limbs after shopping, or for a pre-dinner drink on the armless white leather sofas near the bar. If the sofas are all occupied, then head down the road to the Whitelaw Hotel, which has the same owner and the same vibe. If you don't like armless white leather sofas, then you are in the wrong town.

Sky Bar, The Shore Club, 1901 Collins Avenue, Miami Beach
Tel: 305 695 3100   www.shoreclub.com
Open: 7pm–4am daily

This is one of the top spots of Miami nightlife, attracting the kind of local that has the Miami attitude but is prepared to talk to strangers. Located at the Shore Club hotel, Sky Bar comprises four lounge areas, two of which are bars beside the pool while the other two encircle the Red Bar, which becomes the epicentre of Sky Bar activity from around 11pm. Attending Sky Bar is a selection of young businessmen, a few models and the odd rapper band who make sure the pool area fills with spliff smoke. At the bar, the crowd is friendly, substantially more so than that at Mynt, where people continue to pout way past 3am. By that time at Sky Bar people are too drunk to care. If you plan to come here, it is important to remember two things: dress as stylishly as you can in order to get in, and be sure to use the Shore Club facilities before 11pm when the bouncers put additional velvet ropes across the Red Bar's door and make people wait to get back in, even if you have been drinking there for hours and have a drink waiting for you at the bar. This seems like a pointless exercise, but the management says that it is to ensure the limited space is not crowded out by men, and that the pretty women are left alone for at least a few seconds over the course of the evening when those chatting them up feel the call of nature. Welcome to Miami.

Sofi Lounge, 423 Washington Avenue, Miami Beach
Tel: 305 532 4444 www.sofilounge.com
Open: 9pm–5am daily

Sofi Lounge is located just south of Fifth Avenue, as the name suggests. The interior is dressed in red, decorated with abstract paintings and lit in red as well. This is a bar for locals and people who work in the nearby restaurants and clubs, so when it fills it can be a jolly evening as this kind of South Beach professional makes sure he or she has a good time once they've seen the glitterati get high on the vodka they poured just hours earlier. Sofi Lounge is not cutting-edge South Beach – it's too raw for that; rather it fills late night at the weekends or on a Friday evening, but never early. There is a pool table and happy hour is seven days a week from 3 until 9pm.

Tequila Chicas, 1501 Ocean Drive, South Beach
Tel: 305 531 7010
Open: 11am–4am daily

Only a short walk from the beach, Tequila Chicas is a new Latin bar at the northern tip of Ocean Drive in an arty courtyard that has been crying out for a bar since the last one closed down. It's a dog-eat-dog world in Miami, so at Tequila Chicas they offer some staggering deals on drinks to draw the customers in. The bar itself is a solid, square structure built in stone and topped with wooden surfaces, decorated with baskets full of limes and a blonde bartender who crushes the fruit and grinds the mint. The mood can only be described as tropical and unpretentious. The bar fills in the early evenings as locals get off work or people make their way back from the beach. Tequila Chicas should be open for the foreseeable future as long as the owner does not offer to give the bar away as part of one of his ludicrous drinks

deals. Not necessarily chic, but once the Tequila starts flowing –
God help us all!

**Tiffany Spire Bar, The Hotel, 801 Collins Avenue, South
Beach**
Tel: 305 531 2222 www.thehotelofsouthbeach.com
Open: 7pm–1am Thurs–Sun

This bar has not been exposed to the general public until now.
In 1998 Tiffany the jewellers challenged Tiffany the hotel, which
opened on South Beach in 1939, over the rights to its original
name. The jewellers came out on top, but the hotel was allowed
to keep the famous Tiffany Spire on the roof of the building.

After a period of collective masterminding, developer Tony Goldman and his team renamed the hotel 'The Hotel'. They also fitted a bar at the base of the spire and added some decking and sofas. With views of the entire city, this has to be one of the most idyllic spots to soak in the South Beach experience. The bar is closed at the beginning of the week but hosts Thursday night parties and is popular at weekends. There is also access to The Hotel's roof pool, which is lit up at night.

Vue, Victor Hotel, 1144 Ocean Drive, Miami Beach
Tel: 305 428 1234 www.hotelvictorsouthbeach.com
Open: 5pm–midnight daily

The Victor Hotel opened too late in the early 2005 season for its bar to develop a loyal following, but this is a decadent open-air spot on the hotel's first floor that will be flooded with interest for years to come. Guests lounge back on oversized basket sofas and watch abstract images of jellyfish being projected onto

giant screens, or stand up and peer over the busy Ocean Drive. The female bartender has been working on South Beach for a number of years and is a fountain of knowledge on most topics, including fine dining. A drink here is idyllic after a scorching day on the beach: the place is seductively lit, the music is kept to a good volume and the breeze is soothing. Gianni Versace, who lived next door, used to do exactly the same on the balcony of his beloved mansion.

Notes and Updates...

snack...

Whether it be a quick bite to eat or a leisurely lunch, Miami has something up its sleeve for everyone; everyone, that is, except for those looking for a late night vindaloo or a kebab. The joy of taking time out for a snack in this city is that it can be done at any time of day or night. When they say it's a city that never sleeps, they also mean that it's a place where you can always find something to eat, no matter what time it is.

There are four main options. First, there is the all-American diner, which is best experienced late at night after a night out, in the morning when the most committed clubbers are finally winding down, or a little later when the holiday-makers get up. Miami is not the most American of cities, so if it is your first time in the US, then breakfast at Jerry's Famous Deli or the 11th Street Diner. These are classic diners like those you see in the movies, so try one out at least once, even if it's just to order a malted shake and a stack of pancakes.

Second, there is the mall-side restaurant for recharging tired shopping legs – a great place for scrutinizing people's outfits and figures as they strut by with rat-sized dogs, and for picking up dinner dates. Head to Lincoln Road – the heart of South Beach – where the best for gossip are Segafredo, Tiramesu, Cafeteria and Van Dyke Café. Don't be embarrassed to look people up and down or even

sniff them as they walk by. In fact, they would be disappointed if you didn't, having spent somebody else's wages on the latest beauty products, handbags and shoes. Expect to be scrutinized yourself – so try your hardest to achieve that fresh, yet bleary-eyed look, and for God's sake don't look like a slob.

Thirdly, there is the trendy eaterie, close to the action, but off the beaten track, where you can tuck into hearty helpings of great food alongside locals who will either give you credit for realizing the potential of their hang-out or curse you for invading their territory. They must learn how to share. A La Folie and Ice Box Café top this category.

And finally there are the take-outs, for those who want to munch away on crab claws watching the sun go down on the Miami skyline or come up on Miami Beach, retreat to the hotel room for games of poker, or enjoy a picnic on the beach. Joe's Take Out and Le Sandwicherie produce South Beach's top take-out fare.

Also included here are some more upmarket restaurants that are excellent if a spot of light lunch is what you're after. In Miami lunching out is almost as important as going out for dinner. It's an opportunity for the locals to reflect on the night before, to plan the forthcoming night out, and most of all it's a chance for a gossip. Ago, at the Shore Club, is a must for upper echelon tittle-tattle, while the Courtyard Grill, at the Biltmore, becomes home to golfing widows nursing Bloody Marys.

11th Street Diner, 1065 Washington Avenue, South Beach
Tel: 305 534 6373
Open: 24 hours daily

This spaceship-like diner was uprooted from its original home in Wilkes-Barre, Pennsylvania, in 1948 and reassembled on South Beach. It landed right beside Twist (South Beach's top gay nightclub – see Party) and serves every kind of comfort food imaginable for intoxicated night owls, lady boys and locals who just love their authentic American diner cuisine. Like Jerry's Famous Deli, it's open all day every day, but it's smaller, the staff are friendlier and the food cheaper. Anyway, it's much more fun to sit in a stainless-steel spaceship from Pennsylvania. 11th St Diner is a good place for late-night binges or a hung-over breakfast on the way to the beach.

A la Folie, 516 Española Way, South Beach
Tel: 305 538 4484
Open: 9am–midnight daily

The sight of the French chef at A la Folie wearing a handkerchief over his head may seem a little strange at first. Don't let be deterred. He produces some excellent stuffed crêpes as well as *croques monsieurs* and *madames*. A la Folie is ideal for lunch or an

afternoon snack, and attracts a regular group of locals, who like to revel in a slice of French culture. The décor has a revolutionary theme emboldened with French graffiti, while the tables outside overlook wall paintings of Fidel Castro and Havana. But you will soon forget about Fidel when you meet the owner, who just loves to talk about Paris. The cups of coffee served in enormous soup bowls come as even more of a surprise than the chef's attire, but if you don't fancy coffee, the outdoor lounge area provides an intimate setting for an early evening drink.

Ago, The Shore Club, 1901 Collins Avenue, South Beach
Tel: 305 695 3226 www.agorestaurant.com
Open: 7am–4pm, 7pm–midnight (1am Fri/Sat) daily

At Ago they like to keep things simple and healthy, and receive a fresh supply of olive oil from Italy three times a week. Ago sits beside Nobu at The Shore Club hotel and has a covered outdoor seating area that overlooks the pool. Another Robert de Niro investment on the beach, it's regarded as one of the top Italians in town, but it is best to come during the day when it is less crowded. While the food is delicious, the menu is pretty standard for an Italian that many rank so highly. The interior features a long stylish bar, which although sophisticated is a little reminiscent of an airport lounge, so your best bet is to sit outside with the Shore Club's pool as a backdrop. Enjoy a delicious plate of risotto with prawns and asparagus tips, as well as the in-

house entertainment: toned men performing backflips to impress the lines of girls on the sunbeds only to be admonished by the pool attendants.

Balans, 1022 Lincoln Road, South Beach
Tel: 305 534 9191 www.balans.co.uk
Open: 8am–midnight (1am Fri/Sat) daily

Balans is London's representative on the Beach and is regarded by some to be the ideal café and bar for the closet gay. This place fills with an eclectic mix of people, but under the surface

the gay community see this as a place to meet potential love interests, partly because most of the staff here are gay. Also known to be a little moody, they often behave as though their modelling agents are about to come through the door at any moment waving the next Armani contract, and will pour your club soda while they stare at their reflection in the mirrors along the walls. Balans is therefore a fun place to eat if you know what to expect. The menu offers a range of filling recipes with an Asian or Mediterranean twist, while there is a long bar that attracts all sorts in the evening. As well as a suitable place for breakfast and lunch, Balans is slightly more sophisticated and less in-your-face than Laundry Bar or Score if you're wanting an early drink.

Cafeteria, 546 Lincoln Road, South Beach
Tel: 305 672 3663
Open: 24 hours daily

What was a Cadillac dealership has now become Cafeteria, sister restaurant to the New York branch that every American seems to know about from the television. If you're none the

wiser, however, then expect a modern interior with white leather upholstered seats above which is a stylish frosted and clear glass partition that separates a long bar from the dining area. Outside, the building still carries the Cadillac insignia above the doorway and there are wooden tables under brown umbrellas outside for people-watching. The menu offers dishes such as macaroni cheese, delicious salads and a decent list of cocktails, and there's a jazz lounge at the rear. Be prepared for two types of waiters: those who take orders and serve food, and those who clear the tables. Although it's difficult to tell the difference, the latter tend to get irritated if you ask them questions.

Café Abracci, 318 Aragon Avenue, Coral Gables
Tel: 305 441 0700
Open: 11.30am–2.30pm, 6–11pm (midnight Fri/Sat). Closed Sat/Sun lunch.

Local restaurateurs will tell you that at Café Abracci, the treatment is better than the food. Well, the food is good, but the treatment is excellent if you turn up dressed to match the fine dining setting. Café Abracci (which you can translate as something like 'Hug Café') is like a restaurant in a mobster movie, where gangsters embrace each other before lunch, and then try

to 'whack' each other later in the day. The menu includes all the classic Italian dishes with a few personal additions from the chef. Café Abracci has withstood the ever-changing trends of Florida and will continue to do so because although the food is good, the formal dining setting makes it taste even better. Café Abracci and the Courtyard Grill at the Biltmore are Coral Gables' best options for a lunch in the week.

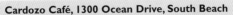

Cardozo Café, 1300 Ocean Drive, South Beach
Tel: 305 695 2822
Open: 8am–midnight (1am Fri/Sat) daily

Cardozo Café is located in the Art Deco Cardozo Hotel at the tranquil northern end of Ocean Drive. Owned by Gloria Estefan, it was built in 1939 by Henry Hohauser and his team who were basically responsible for the area. The Café is a popular spot for breakfast or lunch, as the food here is considerably better than many of its imitators on the stretch – if you are going to spend around $12 for a vegetarian crêpe, you might as well do it at the Cardozo. Guests can either sit in the hotel's lobby area or outside, on one of the wicker chairs or in the shade of the umbrellas that hug the sidewalk. The atmosphere is relaxed until the place becomes busy at lunchtime, so come mid-morning, when a cool breeze blows down Ocean Drive and softens the clout of the Miami heat.

Cavalier, 1320 Ocean Drive, South Beach
Tel: 305 531 3555
Open: 8.30am–midnight daily

Architecturally, the Art Deco Cavalier Hotel is a gem. Built in 1936 and renovated in 1992, the Cavalier is best visited with a quick lunch at their charming café. The restaurant offers some

adventurous Italian fare and is run by some feisty Latino girls and a couple of ultra-friendly Italian waiters. Since their English is not very good, ordering can be an adventure in itself – and that's just part of the charm of the Cavalier. There's no long list of specials, but instead the staff will advise you. Meatballs seem to be the most popular option. They are good, but are a little filling on a hot day when one of their vegetarian sandwiches might be more appropriate.

Courtyard Grill, Biltmore Hotel, 1200 Anastasia Avenue, Coral Gables
Tel: 305 445 8066 www.biltmorehotel.com
Open: 11am–3pm, 5.30–9.30pm daily

Coral Gables should be given serious credit for features such as the Venetian pool and some of the best restaurants in Miami, but surprisingly there are not many places where you can sit outside in the shade and have lunch. Which is why this courtyard, with sunshades ranged round its central fountain, is the top luncheon location in Coral Gables, and is especially useful if you are about to play a round of golf on the Biltmore's 18-hole course. With nine separate food stations, the Courtyard attracts a mixed crowd: tourists who have come to see the hotel; locals who are rich enough to take the afternoon off for some pampering at the spa; and of course the golfers. Do not forget to take a look at

the gigantic pool, which is the most challenging place in Miami to do a length under water. Don't try it after lunch.

Ice Box Café, 1657 Michigan Avenue, South Beach
Tel: 305 538 8448
Open: 11am (10am Sat/Sun)–11pm (midnight Fri/Sat) daily

Ice Box Café is about 40 yards from Lincoln Road – just far enough away not to be flooded with tourists but close enough to gain a religious following of locals and a few visits from those tourists prepared to stray slightly off the beaten track. For such a little café renowned for its counter full of cakes and pastries, its kitchen comes out with some seriously impressive dishes as

well as its signature sweeties such as peanut butter ice-cream cake. The interior is modern yet cosy, with a stainless-steel counter or wooden tables to sit at and a couple of sofas for those waiting for a hangover cure. The South American staff are charming; they quietly natter away amongst themselves about nightclubs and how much they miss Buenos Aires but always serve the customers with a smile.

Jerry's Famous Deli, 1450 Collins Avenue, South Beach
Tel: 305 532 8030 www.jerrysfamousdeli.com
Open: 24 hours daily

It takes a hurricane warning to make Jerry's Famous Deli close its doors. During the last warning, the barman waited at the restaurant until the entire population of South Beach had been evacuated before boarding up the windows. He then went surfing. Jerry's is open 24 hours a day and has over 250 choices on the menu, including the American classics; the committed staff are familiar with most of them, so just name your choice. There are also some sinful puddings on display. Jerry's is set in a former ballroom, but now looks like a quintessential diner with red leather booths and a long bar for those on their own. The place is expensive for what it is, but is an interesting all-American dining experience. Even though it's not flashy, celebrities still sneak in for the occasional pastrami sandwich and soda.

Joe's Take Out, 11 Washington Avenue, South Beach
Tel: 305 673 4611
Open: 11.30am–2.30pm, 5–10pm (11pm Fri/Sat) daily

People flock to Joe's Stone Crab restaurant next door purely for the food: it's not the atmosphere or the service that they crave, they are there for the stone crabs. By going to Joe's Take Out you can avoid the hassle of waiting in line for a table with hordes of hungry Florida folk, and take some delicious stone crabs to the destination of your choice. We recommend the beach at dusk with a bottle of wine. The stone crab claws are placed in ice, so they will be fresh for hours.

Leslie Café, 1244 Ocean Drive, South Beach
Tel: 305 532 7580   www.lesliecafe.net
Open: 8am–10pm (11pm Fri/Sat) daily

The Leslie Café is a relaxing place to soak up the atmosphere on Ocean Drive at breakfast or lunchtime. Housed in a typical Art Deco building, with a row of white curtains tied down at the front, it's just about as romantic a setting as you get on a road where acrylic shorts and white socks pulled up to the knees are the latest in men's fashions. The Leslie quietly exudes that little bit of arrogance that is missing from many of the cafés and

restaurants on Ocean Drive. The menu offers salads, pastas and fresh fish dishes and its prices are consistently reasonable.

Miss Yip Café, 1661 Meridian Avenue, South Beach
Tel: 305 534 5488
Open: midday–11pm (midnight Fri/Sat) daily

Miss Yip Café, located just off Lincoln Road and owned by ambitious New Yorker Jenny Yip, who launched the Blue Door restaurant at the Delano Hotel, offers the best selection of Chinese food on South Beach. Always packed, Miss Yip Café is the kind of place where hotel guests spot their concierge out of uniform and with a pair of chopsticks in his hand at the neighbouring

table. This is not an especially hip venue, but the Hong Kong cuisine cooked by Chinese–born chef Vincent Cheng attracts a diverse crowd who all regularly return. The place is clean, but the dark red leather sofas complemented by the flowery wall paper and smudged mirrors give the interior that ever so shabby-chic feel. Above Miss Yip's is the new, trendy Buck 15 bar, which is a must-see.

Pelican Café, 826 Ocean Drive, South Beach
Tel: 305 673 1000
Open: 8am–12.30am (2am Fri/Sat) daily

If you find yourself at the southern end of Ocean Drive at lunchtime, then the Pelican Café at the Pelican Hotel is the needle in the haystack. Here they are desperate to distinguish themselves from neighbouring restaurants on Ocean Drive that cook a few dishes and leave them out on display to fester all day. At Pelican Café they are looking for the slightly more sophisticated client. There is seating on the pavement, but the Pelican is best enjoyed at the tables just above street level in the day and early evening. The menu is Italian-orientated, with high-quality pastas, salads and sandwiches and caters well for vegetarians. The restaurant is open in the evening and has a smart interior with green and red leather booths. If the Pelican is full, then try the Cardozo, Cavalier or Leslie Café along the Drive.

Puerto Sagua, 700 Collins Avenue, South Beach
Tel: 305 673 1115
Open: 7.30am–2am daily

Surrounded by boutique stores and stylish hotels, the shabby
Puerto Sagua sticks out like a sore thumb on Collins Avenue, but
the quality of its Cuban cuisine means this restaurant is accepted
as part of the furniture on SoBe. Puerto Sagua is a living
reminder that any Cuban who sets foot on American soil cannot
be sent back to Cuba. They have repaid the favour. Anyone who
sets foot in Puerto Sagua will come out satisfied and with change
in their pockets. Rice, beans and meat form a staple part of the
Cuban diet, and thus constitute the basis of the menu. Despite
the basic home-style café décor, this is the best Cuban restaurant around, and many hip locals love to prove that they do not
need lounge chairs, fancy artwork and house music to enjoy a
good breakfast, lunch or dinner. Be aware that Cuban coffee is
very strong, and mixed with some rice, eggs and beans makes
the perfect antidote to the night before.

La Rosinella, 525 Lincoln Road, South Beach
Tel: 305 672 8777
Open: 11am–midnight (1am Fri–Sun) daily

Pretty Colombian waitresses and an elderly Italian lady they call
Mamma greet customers at this Roman trattoria. The man

behind the bar, who claims to make the best espresso in the neighbourhood, also calls her Mamma. He is, in fact, her husband. Family matters aside, La Rosinella opened in 1997 and serves some cracking Italian dishes, all made with ingredients from the local market. La Rosinella is also a good place for dinner, but is best enjoyed during the day, while taking a break from shopping

on Lincoln Road. It is located towards the eastern end of the road (beach side), so most shoppers pass it on their way to the shops and again on the way back to the hotel laden with bags. The food here is well priced, so shopping sprees do not have to be curbed on account of Mamma's kitchen.

Le Sandwicherie, 229 14th Street, South Beach
Tel: 305 532 8934
Open: 9am–5am daily

Having introduced the baguette to South Beach, the French are now busy showing Floridians how to fill it properly with prosciutto and mozzarella at the popular La Sandwicherie. It's worth sitting at the counter just to watch how fast these Frenchmen can stuff these baguettes full of delicious ingredients. Thirty-five seconds remains the current record for a ham, turkey and salad baguette with extra French dressing and jalapenos. You can either sit at the bar, which serves soft drinks (but no alcohol), or order to go. La Sandwicherie is perfect for beach picnickers, for those who have the late-night munchies or for those who just don't

129

want to sit down in a restaurant. Sandwiches are very well filled and can be shared. If the jalapenos have you sweating, look no further than the Club Deuce bar on the other side of the road, which will serve you a cold beer and caters for all fetishes.

Segafredo, 1040 Lincoln Road, South Beach
Tel: 305 673 0047 www.segafredo.it
Open: 11am–2am daily

Either tuck into the Martini list or do it European-style and order a glass of red wine before you judge people's outfits as they strut by. At Segafredo there are no two ways about it: you have to get stuck in and have an opinion on all fashion matters if you are to blend in properly. It's the kind of place where Latin men undo the bow at the back of the waitress's apron and then

snigger behind their menus; where peroxide blondes chainsmoke and talk about Gucci jumpers for their rodent-like dogs; and where you snack on salads, *carpaccio* and *paninis* at lunchtime or after work. It's an Italian coffee bar on the widest catwalk in Miami, and should be paid a visit.

Talula, 210 23rd Street, South Beach
Tel: 305 672 0778 www.talulaonline.com
Open: midday–2.30pm, 6–10.30pm (11.30pm Fri, Sat). Closed Mondays.

The garden area at the back of Talula is ideal for lunch if you are staying at the upper end of South Beach. Situated a little out of the way, the restaurant is popular with those who are not interested in the commerciality of Lincoln Road and crave something different from the ubiquitous Caesar salad. Chefs Andrea Curto-Randazzo and Frank Randazzo run the show, producing contemporary American cuisine. All deliciously cooked, the food is moderately priced for its location. Talula is good for both lunch or dinner and is not particularly well known, which means it can attract those couples who don't want to be seen in public together. A place where affairs can begin and end.

Tapas Y Tintos, 448 Española Way, South Beach
Tel: 305 538 8272
Open: midday–1am (5am Sat/Sun) daily

For an early evening snack or light dinner, look no further than Tapas y Tintos, the Spanish *tapas* bar that gets packed with Spaniards who love their Gypsy Kings, red wine and, as you would expect, *tapas*. Located on Española way, it is actually the closest thing to España on the stretch. Forget the other tacky Mexican and eclectic restaurants (except Hosteria Romana, which is equally tacky but serves decent food) and come here, where you can perch at the bar or lounge at a table listening to live music. This place is always packed, so reservations are necessary if you intend to go all out and dine here; otherwise, just turn up for some *tapas* and *tintos* at the bar before heading off to a more serious dining location.

Tiramesu, 721 Lincoln Road, Miami Beach
Tel: 305 532 4538 www.tiramesu.com
Open: midday–midnight (1am Fri, Sat) daily

If you ask the South Beach locals where they like to go and eat in the day, many will say Tiramesu. They see it for what it is: a no-nonsense restaurant that produces a high standard of Italian cuisine, quickly and at a reasonable price. But most of all they respect its consistency and its ability to draw in fashionable locals. Inside the restaurant has a sizeable bar and a dining room with some funky modern art on the walls, but it is best to sit outside, not directly in front of the building, but in the shaded area on the other side of the walkway where there is more space and less danger of a rollerblader crashing into your table.

Centrally located on Lincoln Road, it is ideal for lunch or a
recharging cappuccino during shopping.

The Van Dyke Café, 846 Lincoln Road, Miami Beach
Tel: 305 534 3600
Open: 8.30am–2am daily

A music lounge and café, like Cafeteria, the Van Dyke is popular
with tourists. The 1924 Van Dyke building towers above everything but the Sony headquarters and the Sun Trust Bank (which
is also a good place to get cash out at the Western end) on
Lincoln Road and is covered in creeper, which is quite a refreshing change from the concrete walls of most of the buildings
along the road. The ground floor is dedicated to the café, offering
burgers, salads, omelettes and pizzas, while the upstairs is the
jazz bar which plays live jazz seven nights a week. The Van Dyke
is a good pit stop for shoppers and boasts Miami's only jazz bar.

party...

There is a distinct possibility that you will leave Miami with memory loss. Welcome to the fashion show that never sleeps, to the city where you can drink Martinis and mojitos shoulder-to-shoulder with models, movie stars and self-acclaimed superstars – provided the doorman lets you slip past the velvet ropes, that is.

The party is the king of the Miami scene, but you have to know where to go on what night. Turning up at the Astor's Metro Bar on a Tuesday will find you drinking with SoBe's nocturnal aristocracy, but on Fridays expect out-of-towners trying to ride the wave.

Dress as cool as you can. What this means is anyone's guess. Guys – put on anything that has a label, make sure your gold chain is showing and put a sock in your underwear. It's hard being a man in Miami; forced to buy the drinks, persecuted at the door if not accompanied by at least three girls and then blown out for a boy with a Lamborghini. To try and guarantee yourself entry, ask your concierge to put you on the guest list. Otherwise you'll just have to pretend they should be paying you to come in. With that attitude, you'll either be welcomed with open arms and ushered into the VIP lounge where you'll be forcefed vodka before being handed a bill in excess of your monthly mortgage payments, or you'll find yourself staring hopefully from the pavement with the rest of the night's wannabes.

Girls have it rather easier than men in Miami. Here girls rule. Put some extensions in your hair and wear as little as you can without being pulled over by the cops for public indecency, and you should be fine. Girls in Miami dress to show off, quite literally, so do not be afraid to reveal a little flesh and treat men as if you own them. Never pay for a drink and if you are looking for that long-lost sugar daddy, there is a strong possibility that he may be sitting in one of Miami's lounges, lonely, sharing out his $400 bottle of vodka to a few girls who are paid to encourage him to buy more, waiting for you to sit on his knee.

In South Beach the party scene is dominated by lounges and then lounges within lounges, and who gets into which VIP lounge varies from place to place. There are some totally insane policies and as always the buck is king – the more cash you are prepared to drop, the more exclusive you become. Your problem will then be the company you find yourself in, which might not be the most pleasant in town (although the young and the hip do manage to slip in).

On South Beach Mynt is always popular and at the time of writing is the club of choice for all. In the Design District a similar lounge experience to SoBe is on offer, and you need not really look beyond Pawn Shop, Grass or I/O. Finally in the Downtown area, book yourself into rehab ahead of time. Space and Nocturnal are the two main locations and party way beyond the early hours. Pop into Club Envy for after hours.

On a **Monday** there is no safer option than Tantra's Goddess party, or, if you are up for a gritty evening, head to the Backdoor Bamby party at Crobar, a legendary weekly mixed gay/straight party often touted as the best party of the week. Otherwise there is always B.E.D.'s secret society party.

The trickiest day is **Tuesday**. The safest bet is to go to Rumi, which is also open for dinner (while the hippest crowd goes to the Astor hotel's Metro Bar to party first).

On **Wednesday** both B.E.D. and Jimmy'z (after dinner at the Forge) take their turn, hosting their flagship events, while Mynt and Tantra also open their doors.

On **Thursday** the Miami weekend begins. Amika should be your first choice, but you also can take your pick from Onda Lounge, which is becoming popular, Mansion and Privé. Away from South Beach are Pawn Shop and Grass.

Fridays and **Saturdays** the Miami nightclub showdown begins. You will be spoiled for choice on South Beach as all clubs will be open. This may well be a suitable time to sample the Miami rave experience in Nocturnal and Space.

On **Sundays** don't forget the unbelievably sexy Raleigh pool party in the afternoon, after which look no further than Nikki Beach or Pearl at the southern end of South Beach. They are in the same building, but Nikki Beach, which has dubbed itself 'the sexiest place on Earth', does not take any prisoners and gets started by the late afternoon.

Amika, 1532 Washington Avenue, South Beach
Tel: 305 534 1499 www.amikamiami.com
Open: 9pm–5am Thurs–Sun

Amika is a new SoBe haunt, owned and operated by Miami
native Tony Guerra, who claims to be one of the most popular
nightclub figures on the Beach. The motto here is 'amicable
venue', but in truth the 'let's be friendly' policy is only really
extended to those who spend oodles of cash. There are so many
roped-off areas that everyone who doesn't make the A-list is left
with only three measly bar areas to party in. Your best bet here
is to book a table and buy a couple of bottles – after all, if you
go to Miami, you have to be prepared to invest in nocturnal
activities. However you justify it, they will happily relieve you of
any excess pocket money. Amika is a suitable alternative to Mynt
on South Beach, drawing in the same crowd.

B.E.D., 929 Washington Avenue, South Beach
Tel: 305 532 9070 www.bedmiami.com
Open: 8.30pm–5am. Closed Tuesdays and Sundays.

Although B.E.D. is apparently an abbreviation for Beverage,
Entertainment and Dining, there are no prizes for guessing what
the main theme is here. The room is full of beds that can each
take about 10 people, who lean on mountains of cushions against

the wall or just lie down. B.E.D. does serve dinner, the 'first lay' beginning at 8.30pm and the second at 10.30pm, the idea being to eat as the Romans did back in the day when South Beach was still a swamp. B.E.D. wakes up from 11pm when the doors open to non-diners. Monday's 'Secret Society' hip-hop and R&B night is the club's busiest night and also the hardest to get into, which is when concierges earn their keep by managing to put you on the guest list. The 'In bed with' Wednesday parties are also popular. There is a 'fashionably hip and chic' dress code, so save the Green Flash trainers for Space or Nocturnal on the weekend. Along with Mynt and Tantra, B.E.D. attracts Miami's A-list.

Cafeteria Lounge, 560 Lincoln Road, South Beach
Tel: 305 672 3663
Open: 6pm–2am daily

Walk to the back of Cafeteria restaurant and glide through a space-age walkway to find Cafeteria Lounge – a stylish but more intimate alternative to the front-line venues of Miami. The Lounge has a central bar and private dens at the back kitted out with sofas and round tables, while the curved DJ booth blends in as another bar, serving up a mix of chill-out lounge beats and house tunes. The egg-shaped chairs and illuminated mirrors continue the decorative theme of the restaurant in a nocturnal setting. Even though Cafeteria restaurant is a magnet for tourists who have seen Cafeteria in New York, Cafeteria Lounge is known more by locals than tourists because it is not visible from Lincoln Road. Come here for a few drinks and a warm-up dance before hitting more serious club destinations.

Crobar, 1445 Washington Avenue, South Beach
Tel: 305 672 8084   www.crobarmiami.com
Open: 10pm–5am Mon, Thurs–Sat

Formerly the Cameo Theatre built in 1938, Crobar still attracts some eye-opening costumes and some not-so-talented actors, including a regular crowd of shemales. The kinky 'Backdoor Bamby' party on Monday nights is always popular, as anything seems to go, attracting both the gay and straight communities. On Fridays and Saturdays Crobar fills with tourists as well as a

slightly more relaxed breed of Miamian for its trance and house sessions. Crobar is another club to take its VIP policy to unnecessary levels by grading just how very important a person you are. Not content with having a VIP lounge, they have gone all-out and added a Super VIP section. What you have to do to get in there is 'classified'. Crobar is the centre of decadence on Miami Beach. For the hungry clubber there is a Pizza Rustica next door.

Grass, 28 NE 40th Street, Design District
Tel: 305 573 3355 www.grasslounge.com
Open: 7.30pm–3am. Closed Sundays.

Although it would be impossible to eliminate exposed silicone breasts and hardcore techno from Miami, at Grass they are keeping things real with the chill-out music turned down low – until after dinner when the Gestapo-like doormen decide who is pert enough to get in. Grass is an ultra-trendy restaurant and lounge that sits between two buildings in the Design District. The setting is a cross between Indonesian and Caribbean as palm-thatched huts cover the centrepiece bar, around which are

low-slung tables and cushioned chairs. To avoid being trampled on after dinner at the low tables by the bar, book a booth, as this is when Miami's pretty boys and girls flick their fringes back, put their 'Blue Steel' faces on and make their entrance for the night's main event. The dancing and drinking then gets faster until 3am, when it is time to move on.

I/O, 30 NE 14th Street, at North Miami Avenue, Downtown
Tel: 305 358 8007 www.iolounge.com
Open: 10pm–5am Thurs–Sat

Located in the design district in a pretty dodgy area (so do not park your hired Hummer unless you tip a vigilante) I/O is Miami's top underground location to see live music, hosting shows for up and coming outfits and touring bands (the Brazilian Girls played what is now seen as a legendary gig at I/O and are now a household name in New York and have played in Central Park). I/O is split up into three sections: a seriously long bar where the men wait to be served before they head back into the main room where thirsty music lovers watch the bands, and finally an outside terrace for non smokers and stargazers. Saturday Night Poplife sessions attract a loyal following of locals as the resident dj's spin a mix ranging from Indie Rock to Electro Pop. I/O is not glamorous, but is a creditable location as it's still reasonably unknown by the masses and because some high quality musicians play here.

Jimmy'z, 432 41st Street, Mid Beach
Tel: 305 604 9798 www.theforge.com
Open: 10pm–5am Wed–Sun

Jimmy'z is attached to The Forge restaurant (see Eat), and

accessed through the lobby or the front of the building. Originally a cigar lounge until The Forge's owner Shareef Malnik teamed up with nightlife queen Regine, Jimmy'z is now one of the hottest places to be on a Wednesday night. Entrance is guaranteed if you eat at The Forge. Otherwise Thursday is 'Brazilian Dirty Dancing', Friday is 'Ballroom 41' and Saturday is the 'International World Beat' session. Since The Forge is a Miami

institution it appears in many of the guidebooks, and therefore often attracts an out-of-town crowd – who then continue the evening in Jimmy'z. Entry to the VIP lounge is almost imperative to get past the happy bridge-and-tunnel crowd at the main bar.

Mansion, 1235 Washington Avenue, South Beach
Tel: 305 532 1525   www.mansionmiami.com
Open: 11pm–5am Tues, Thurs–Sat

The majority of the clubbers who frequent Mansion look as if they have come straight off a porn set. This may sound harsh, but – unfortunately, or fortunately, depending on how you look at it, it's a pretty fair assessment. Mansion sums up what Miami is about. It's about packing 2,500 Barbies and Kens into six VIP areas and five dance rooms, charging them $20 to get in, charging them $10 a drink and cranking up the house music until 5am – a couple of hours after the celebrities have wobbled off home in their Hummers. Set in a building that was first built as the

French Casino in 1936, Mansion spans over 40,000 square feet and is tarted up with chandeliers, fireplaces, Venetian mirrors, keystone arches and seven projection screens. Tables can be reserved in advance, ranging from $200 to $2,000 in price, depending on the size of party. If you can't get in, then head across the street to Automatic Slims.

Mynt Ultra Lounge, 1921 Collins Avenue, South Beach
Tel: 786 276 6132
Open: 11pm–5am Wed–Sat

If you want to see the most beautiful girls on South Beach drinking vodka in Russian proportions and dancing around Miami's insanely wealthy, there to pick up the bill, then go to Mynt. If you dress well, arrive with a couple of tallish girls and believe you are

a superstar, getting in will go smoothly. Act like you belong among the celebs; otherwise you will be relegated to the ranks of the autograph hunters outside. Once inside, you'll find three isles of cream sofas laden with girls (some of whom are allegedly there to earn a cut on booze sales) and their sugar daddies. Proceedings are overlooked by a DJ who grinds out the latest house and trance tracks. Further back is Mynt's hip-hop department in a cramped mini lounge filled with some of the town's more attractive figures. If you can afford it, book a table, buy a few bottles of vodka, hire a bouncer and wait for the girls to sit on your knee. If this is all a bit much, then go next door to Rok Bar.

Nikki Beach, I Ocean Drive, South Beach
Tel: 305 538 1111 www.nikkibeach.com
Open: 11pm–5am Mon, Fri, Sat; 3–11pm Sun

If ever you are going to drink a mojito, this is your moment. Located on the southern end of South Beach, Nikki Beach was once dubbed the sexiest place on Earth. Now it's a little passé,

opening its doors to the people who were not quite cool enough to get in a year ago (which basically means most people) – but it's still the sexiest place in Miami. The Sunday Indio Loco ('crazy Indian') party is Nikki Beach's trademark event, luring people off the beaches to chill out on carved round benches padded with white pillows, on hammocks and in private love dens on stilts; meanwhile the house beats are pumped out by the DJ and the drinks are served by male and female staff in special Nikki Beach sarongs. Arrive around 5pm on a Sunday afternoon to enjoy Nikki Beach and pop upstairs to Pearl when it gets dark. Alternatively, this is a good place for lunch.

Nocturnal, 50 NE 11th Street, Downtown
Tel: 877 258 2847 www.nocturnalmiami.com
Open: 10pm–5am Wed–Sat

One of America's most anticipated nightclub venues, Nocturnal is a brand new 20,000-square-foot state-of-the-art mega club spread over three floors. After two years of planning, Nocturnal was finally opened in May 2005 and has not disappointed so far. The first floor houses a main dance-floor with three bars, the second has a balcony overlooking the dance-floor, and the third is a custom-built terrace for clubbers who come up or down to the sunset on the Miami skyline. Add into the mixer the most elaborate sound and lighting system known to man and enormous screens showing images of the crowd going mad to the DJ's trance tunes, and you have a good idea of what to expect. It is unlikely that Nocturnal will threaten Space's dominance in the

Downtown area; rather it enhances Downtown's reputation as the 'baddest' place in Miami, making the lounges of South Beach

look rather tame.

Therapy Thursdays are hot at Onda Lounge, a new location on Washington Avenue. Onda ('good vibe' in Spanish) is owned by Jacquelynn Powers, of renowned *Ocean Drive* magazine, and Michael Pasqualini. The club itself is very similar to many Miami lounge haunts, offering big curving sofas in its VIP area, a couple of bars and a dance-floor – nothing out of the ordinary, then. Onda Lounge's popularity therefore relies on the social noose of the owners to draw in as many important figures as they can. For now, this ploy seems to be working, but the owners are keen to fill the walls. For a less energetic evening, Felt pool bar sits beside Onda Lounge and offers a more relaxed kind of therapy.

Opium Garden, 136 Collins Avenue, South Beach
Tel: 305 531 5535 www.opiummiami.com
Open: 10.30pm–5am Wed–Sun

The garden area at Opium is an open-air courtyard filled with golden Buddhas, Chinese lanterns, opium-den love seats and a centrepiece dance-floor overlooked by cushioned steps. The overall impression is of an exotic amphitheatre which turns dancing into a spectator sport as groovers may be surveyed from the steps above, preventing the phoneys from getting away with jogging on the spot. But if you're too cool to care who is watching, or if you really are good on the dance-floor and want to impress, then Opium is the place to come. Music ranges from hip-hop to house. Beyond the garden is a second level with additional bars and a long lounge area. Opium's VIP area is now run as a separate entity called Privé that has its own entrance (see page 148), but although you can get to it up the steps on the left-hand side of the dance-floor it's almost impossible to get in this way. Ring ahead to get yourself on the guest list for Opium, as the usual strict door policies apply here.

Pawn Shop 1222 NE 2nd Avenue, Design District
Tel: 305 373 3511   www.thepawnshoplounge.com
Open: 10pm–5am daily

Created by Miami's nightlife veteran Kurt Van Nostrand, this former 1930s pawn shop is now the Design District's most popular play-pen for nocturnal activity. The yellow building is covered in classic pawn-shop notices such as 'We buy gold', while the entrance is fronted with bars. The interior is best known for its yellow school bus and its jet fuselage that have been converted into VIP areas. Everything from rock to house is played at Pawn Shop and the club attracts many of Miami's top party queens, some of whom find it necessary to park their Ferraris just yards from the door where lines of hopefuls queue up outside. The bunk beds and retro sofas, which may well have been plucked out of skips, give Pawn Shop that 1970s feeling. To get on the guest list, telephone the club or submit names online.

Pearl Restaurant and Champagne Lounge, 1 Ocean Drive, South Beach
Tel: 305 538 1111
Open: 7pm–5am. Closed Mondays and Tuesdays.

Pearl's round bar surrounded by high-backed seashell chairs is perhaps the most futuristic design in Miami and one of the most satisfying areas to land a seat. The room is decorated entirely in orange and white with polka-dot tables and a wall of bubbling water lit by purple lighting. Pearl serves a souped-up menu of scallops and sushi, but is best known for its lounge, which attracts the usual beach volleyball players, bikini models and model scouts. After dinner a central bar serves champagne to diners, while the main bar area begins to fill at the back. This is where the real action happens at Pearl as South Beach's most attractive exchange make-up tips and tales of the catwalk. Above them Latin American dancers mount the DJ's stage and shake their behinds until the crowd drinks enough and spits out a few intoxicated customers to join them on the bar. The music then gets louder, the drinks continue to flow and the rest is a blur.

Privé, 136 Collins Avenue, Miami Beach
Tel: 305 531 5535 www.opiummiami.com
Open: 11pm–5am Thurs–Sun

You don't have to speak French to work out that local promoters Ingrid Casares and Michael Capponi have made Privé one of the most difficult clubs to get into. Privé is effectively the Opium Garden's VIP area, but you can enter via a separate entrance at the front of the building. The area does have access to Opium's open-air amphitheatre dance-floor area, but has gradually become a separate entity. Streamlined leather sofas and black-

and-white Helmut Newton photographs help to promote an air of exclusivity. Entering through Opium Garden is an almost impossible task, so the trick is to get on the guest list by asking your concierge to ring ahead or to turn up with a mixed group of attractive, well-dressed friends.

Rumi, 330 Lincoln Road, Miami Beach
Tel: 305 672 4353 www.rumimiami.com
Open: 10pm–5am Tues–Sat

Do not be discouraged by the fact that Bill Clinton once partied here. He chose well. Some people say that he was interested in how the club came to be named after a 13th-century Sufi mystic. Others say that he likes to visit former shoe shops. Whatever the truth may be, it's more than likely that once through the door he would have been intrigued by Rumi's blend of restaurant, lounge and club that fills with a fun, young and attractive mix of Miami locals and tourists. This long, narrow space has a

bar and dining room on the ground floor, while the upper level is divided up into a fireplace room for dancing, a second bar and round leather booths and sofas for chilling. The two levels are cleverly blended together by a cluster of suspended rectangle lampshades that hover in between the two floors and cleverly break up the height of the room. Rumi is the perfect place for after dinner speaking.

Space, 34 NE 11th Street, Downtown
Tel: 305 372 9378 www.clubspace.com
Open: 10pm–10am Fri, Sat

Get your glow sticks out of the freezer and slot them in the
suitcase beside the sunglasses and tight vest. It's a good thing
that Downtown Miami is a deserted place on a Sunday morning
because the rooftop sunrise session on the terrace at Space
cranks out the trance beats until mid-morning. Downtown is the
only part of Miami that issues 24-hour liquor licences, and at the
weekends Space is its answer to Ibiza, attracting the 'Royal
Family of Djs'. Deep Dish, Danny Tenaglia, Tiesto and Paul Van

Dyk are regulars, while Paul Oakenfold, Sasha and John Digweed
also make guest appearances. The main dance-floor is surrounded by bars, illuminated by state-of-the-art lighting systems and
overlooked by the VIPs in the upper mezzanine level, and there's
a rooftop terrace for sunrise lovers on the second floor with
two further VIP areas. To be added to the VIP admission list, go
to Space's website. Leave the white gloves at home, though;
apparently they went out of fashion years ago.

**Tantra, 1445 Pennsylvania Avenue, at Espanola Way,
South Beach**
Tel: 305 672 4765 www.tantrarestaurant.com
Open: 7pm–5am daily

Russian models like to dance on the tables here, it has been discovered. This is the place where you go for an overpriced but
tasty dinner and later as many cocktails that you can drink without falling down on the grass floor. Like Pearl, Tantra turns into a
full-on party scene after pudding, as guests get up from their
tables and head towards the turf-covered bar area. The lanterns
in the dining room are, however, causing concern among Asian
clients who recognize them as funeral lamps. Whatever the cul-
tural mix-up, Monday nights at Tantra are now etched into the

Miami socialite calendar and draw the same crowd as the Metro
bar on Tuesdays. Drinks at Tantra, however, are a little more rau-
cous as girls dance on any surface they can find that is not occupied by cocktails and the cramped bar area fills to the brim
while couples are turned away by the bouncers outside.

GAY CLUBS

Crème, above Score, 725 Lincoln Lane, Miami Beach
Tel: 305 535 1111 www.cremelounge.net
Open: 10pm–5am daily

Crème Lounge is the remodelled upstairs section of Score with
an entrance on Lincoln Lane. It looks like most lounges in Miami,
with leather sofas and soft coloured lighting – the only
differences being that it fills with men and the sugar daddies are

surrounded by house boys and twinkies instead of silicone girls. Thursday night is 'Crème and Sugar' night, which is part of the Lincoln Lane Block party with Laundry Bar and Buck 15. The music is a mixture of house, trance and hip-hop.

Jade Lounge, 1766 Bay Road, South Beach
Tel: 305 538 7876
Open: 9am–5am Fri–Sun

Located just around the corner from Purdy Lounge and a Harley Davidson rental, Jade is a two-storey bar and nightclub that packs them in on a Friday night for the gay session. The bar on the ground floor stays open all day at the weekend, but South Beach

visitors are attracted to the giant den on the first floor which becomes one of the most crowded, sweaty locations on the beach (which is exactly why many men love it). The lounge has a bar at the end of the room and is filled with cushions, beds and sofas for chilling. For a night of Roman decadence, look no further than Jade.

Laundry Bar, 721 Lincoln Lane, South Beach
Tel: 305 531 7700 www.laundrybar.com
Open: 7am–5am daily

The idea behind Laundry Bar is simple: put your clothes in the machine, drink a beer, play a game of pool and meet some fellow washermen. If you don't have any clothes to wash, then you are still welcome. Just off Lincoln Road on Lincoln Lane, Laundry Bar is a full-service laundromat and bar in one that stays open 22 hours a day. It's mainly gay-orientated and is busy every night, with Thursdays and Saturdays proving the most popular. (Thursday nights Laundry Bar takes part in the Lincoln Lane Block party with Buck 15 and Crème.) There is never a cover charge and happy hour is from 4 to 9pm daily when two-for-one drinks are on offer. Everyone is welcome.

Palace, 1200 Ocean Drive, South Beach
Tel: 305 531 9077
Open: 10am–midnight daily

You can't miss Palace on Ocean Drive. Not because the gay community's multicoloured striped flag flutters beside the bar and an all-male group occupies the open-fronted bar area, but because during the day it is normally the most jolly place on Ocean Drive. At Palace, gay literally means happy. Sit on one of the metallic stools on the raised level of the bar and watch the people walk by or brave the tables and stools on the pavement (watch out for stray rollerbladers!). The atmosphere is always cheerful at Palace and it's a fun pit-stop for a snack and a few drinks in the heart of Ocean Drive. The gay section of the beach is located dead ahead, right in line with Palace.

Score, 727 Lincoln Road, South Beach
Tel: 305 535 1111
Open: 3pm–5am daily

The name does not leave much to the imagination. Score is recognizable on Lincoln Road by the large black and red target logo painted onto the entrance. As well as a nightclub, Score is a suitable place for the afternoon drinker, opening its doors at 3pm. The club itself is divided into two parts, a front bar that features some bizarre smoke paddles on the ceiling designed to gently mix up the air, and a bar that overlooks the dance-floor. Score opens its doors to both gay and straight, but the vast majority of the clients are there to meet someone of the same sex. Score remains one of the bastions of the gay community on South

Beach. The male staff, dressed in tight black wife-beaters and hot pants, are living evidence of this.

Twist, 1057 Washington Avenue, South Beach
Tel: 305 538 9478 www.twistsobe.com
Open: 1pm–5am daily

Do not be alarmed if you see men adjusting their dresses outside. Originally a small, dark bar, Twist is now the biggest and best gay club in Miami, boasting six rooms, all of which look like separate nightclubs, a bungalow bar that opens at the weekend and gaiety dancers who perform seven nights a week. With a reduced number of venues to choose from, Twist has become the flag bearer of the gay community, or what's known as the gay

stronghold on the Beach. Twist is not just limited to the evenings, offering two-for-one drinks from 1pm until 9pm – probably the most generous happy hour deal around. The rooms at Twist span two floors and play a mixture of house, hip-hop and trance, in the same style as most nightclubs and lounges on South Beach. The atmosphere is always very friendly, and it is not uncommon for groups of girls to party at Twist to avoid any pushy men. Cross dressers are also welcome. The 11th Street Diner (see Snack) is next door for an after-Twist snackette.

STRIP CLUBS

Club Madonna, 1527 Washington Avenue, South Beach
Tel: 305 534 2000 www.clubmadonna.com
Open: 6pm–5am daily

Club Madonna is the only serious stripping establishment on South Beach. Look for a large window with a woman sitting on a throne inside and a stretch limo with strippers painted on to it. Madonna's has one main room with a central stage and two additional mini stages, with seating areas around them. The girls are not renowned for their beauty, but given the distinct lack of options on South Beach, Madonna's is popular, mainly with tourists. Be sure to look at your credit card bill at the end of the evening, and be warned that hiring the VIP room is not advised.

Solid Gold, 2355 NE 163rd Street, Miami
Phone: 305 956 5726 www.solidgoldvip.com
Open: 3pm (8pm Sat/Sun)–6am daily

It's a 15-minute drive from South Beach, but Solid Gold is widely regarded as the finest gentleman's club in the area, catering for both men and women, gay and straight. If you want to see men, turn left at the entrance, for women turn right. Of the three adult entertainment establishments listed here, the girls that work at Solid Gold are the closest to what would be described as erotic dancers. Guests are escorted to sofas with a view of the stage, although there is seating around the stage from which men attach money to girls. They are currently looking for dancers. No experience is necessary.

Tootsies Cabaret, 19839 NW 2 Ave (441), North Miami
Tel: 305 651 5822 www.tootsiescabaret.com
Open: midday–5am daily

Classy is not a word that springs to mind when you're having your passport photocopied at the door. Tootsies is the most graphic strip club in Miami. It looks like a fast-food joint, serving beer and tacos, but the dozens of naked girls walking around the stage remind customers why they paid $5 to get in. There is nothing left to the imagination at Tootsies: the room is well lit and the dancers, who weren't really wearing much to begin with anyway, get down from the stage after their act and give clients on the front row a close-up in return for one-dollar bills. Tootsies is not so much seedy, it's just honest. The wheel of friction competition, when the evening's host spins a giant wheel to decide which lucky customer wins the 'jackpot', is the highlight!

GAY STRIP CLUBS

Cupid's Cabaret, 1060 NE 79th Street, Downtown
Tel: 305 756 2649 www.cupidscabaret.com
Open: 7pm–5am daily

Cupid's is the Beach's premiere all-male, all-nude strip bar where clients enjoy performances by dancers from all over the world who take off everything but their bow ties. There are booths close to the stage where you can close the curtains for private dances.

culture...

Exploring Miami's culture means discovering a mixture of elements that combine to create the picture that makes up the city. Its population is a blend of South Americans, Cubans, a strong Jewish community and finally that all-American component, which hosts all of these great cultures. Sightseeing here, therefore, can prove fascinating.

In 1959 the Cuban revolution saw around 100,000 refugees rush to the city, the general rule being that any Cuban who set foot on American soil would be given asylum. In 1973 there were nearly 300,000 Cubans in Miami, and in 1980 another 125,000 arrived, many of whom were looked on by Fidel Castro as the unwanted mass of Cuban society. He then looked on as Miami became the murder capital of the US, with over 600 drug-related deaths in 1981. The drug gangs were finally eliminated and the Cuban population has continued to flourish here, with 'Calle Ocho' becoming the focal point of Cuban society, and now the place to go for a taste of Cuban (see Little Havana). Today you can still see chess played and the cigars rolled.

In addition to the Cuban population, there are also large Jewish communities. The Jewish population grew considerably in the 1970s, particularly in Miami's Aventura district. Visit the Ziff Jewish Museum on South Beach, and the Holocaust memorial, *The Sculpture of Love and Anguish*.

At the other end of the scale, Coral Gables is like a different city. It is one of the US's first planned communities and is immediately distinguishable because of its European-style architecture. It is worth a morning out to walk around the district, but if you're pressed for time just get to the Venetian pool or the Biltmore Hotel. The Lowe Museum, attached to Miami's university, is the state's most important art gallery and houses a superb collection drawing pieces from all parts of the world and all periods.

Finally to the apparently cultureless district on South Beach, where more than 800 Art Deco buildings still stand from the 1930s and '40s. Among the buildings are some of Florida's top art centres, including Britto Central (base of Brazilian artist Romero Britto), and the Bass Museum of Art. South Beach, is the US's

stamp on Miami, which means there are now thousands of people from all over the world living in an American Art Deco masterpiece. But smoke a Cuban cigar while walking around the Jewish museum in the heart of the American Art Deco district and wait for the Brazilian security guard to extinguish it. The only truly American things here are the Art Deco buildings and the Coca-Cola signs.

Essentially a party city Miami is not renowned for its culture, so pop along to a gallery, wander around the Vizcaya Gardens or check out Little Havana — it goes some way to assuaging the culture guilt.

Art Center South Florida, 800 Lincoln Road, South Beach
Tel: 305 674 8278 www.artcentersf.org
Open: 1–10pm (11pm Thurs–Sun) daily

When you're in Lincoln Road, make time to pop into this art centre. It's non-profit and is divided up into small, subsidized studio exhibitions by up-and-coming artists. Some of Miami's most interesting young talent works here, and as a gallery structure isn't in place prices are kept low. Visitors can enter the studios when the artists are there, and their art is often for sale.

Bass Art Museum, 2121 Park Avenue, South Beach
Tel: 305 673 7530 www.bassmuseum.org
Open: 10am (11am Sun)–5pm. Closed Mondays and holidays.

The Bass was founded in 1963 when the City of Miami Beach accepted the gift of the art collection of John and Johanna Bass. It is now the epicentre of South Beach's art scene. The museum occupies what was originally the Miami Beach Public Library, which was designed in 1930 by Russell Pancoast, grandson of Miami Beach pioneer John A. Collins. The collection includes European masters, 18th-century English portraits, Chinese art and Flemish tapestries. The museum regularly exhibits three different travelling collections at the same time.

Bay of Pigs Museum, 1821 SW 9th Street, Little Havana
Tel: 305 649 4719
Open: 9am–5pm. Closed Sundays.

The Bay of Pigs Museum tells the story of how Cuban exiles in Miami were trained by the CIA for a top secret mission to invade Cuba in April 1961. The 1,300-strong force was met by the Cuban army after landing in the Bay of Pigs (Bahia de Cochinos). Around 100 were killed, and the rest were captured and imprisoned. Gloria Estefan's father was one of the men captured. The survivors returned to the US in 1962.

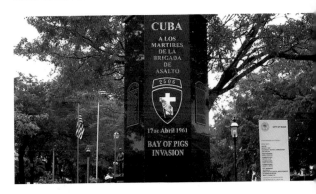

Britto Central, 818 Lincoln Road, South Beach
Tel: 305 531 8821   www.britto.com
Open: 10am–11pm (midnight Fri/Sat) daily

After spending his youth painting on scraps of cardboard and newspapers in Recife, Brazil, Romero Britto travelled to the United States in 1987 to pursue a career in art. Since then his Pop Art has been displayed in over 100 galleries around the world, and most famously on a special-edition Pepsi can. The Miami gallery is Britto's headquarters and, conveniently, the gallery is located on Lincoln Road.

Holocaust Memorial, 1933 Meridian Avenue, South Beach
Tel: 305 538 1663   www.holocaustmmb.org

This powerful memorial is dedicated to the 6 million Jewish victims of the Holocaust. It was commissioned in 1985 and executed by Kenneth Treister, sculptor, who has described it as: 'a large environmental sculpture... a series of outdoor spaces in which the visitor is led through a procession of visual, historical and emotional experiences with the hope that the totality of the visit will express, in some small way, the reality of the Holocaust. The dominant image is the large, 42-foot-high bronze hand, *The Sculpture of Love and Anguish*, which includes an Auschwitz number on the forearm and 130 human figures cast in bronze in various forms of anguish.

Little Havana

After Fidel Castro came to power in 1959, thousands of Cubans fled to US shores. Little Havana is the Cuban capital of Miami, and the street commonly known as Calle Ocho (SW 8th Street) is the place to go and soak up some Cuban culture, drink some strong coffee, and watch the elderly Cubans play chess and puff on a freshly made cigar. The street does now have a McDonald's and several other beautifully constructed fast-food establishments that slightly dilute the authenticity of the place, but this is as Cuban as it gets in Miami and here the Cubans are living their American dream.

Lowe Museum, 1301 Stanford Drive, Coral Gables
Tel: 305 284 3536 www.lowemuseum.org
Open: 10am (midday Thurs, Sun)–5pm (7pm Thurs). Closed
Mondays.

The Lowe is the University of Miami's art museum. Having
opened in 1952 to become the first stand-alone art museum in
Southern Florida, the Lowe is now the most important museum
in the state. The collection, now numbering around 13,000
pieces, draws pieces from ancient Rome and Greece, Native
American and Asian art, Latin America, Africa, classical European
painting, 19th century American art, photography and the contemporary and modern. This eclectic mix is continually expand-
ing and is complemented by continually changing temporary
exhibits. The Lowe has been lucky to attract the support of the
wealthier residents of Miami, whose generosity has allowed the
museum to thrive and grow for the enjoyment and education of
the local population and the university students. If the weather's
wet – why not learn a little?

Maximo Gomez Park, Little Havana

This is the place where old Cubans hang out and play chess. It is
definitely worth going to watch these guys fight it out. They sip
on their insanely strong coffee, puff on seriously long cigars and

play some advanced chess or dominoes. The signs in Spanish will tell you that no spitting or swearing is allowed in the park, so check whether you like the coffee you bought down the street before you walk in.

Vizcaya Museum and Gardens, 3251 South Miami Avenue, Coconut Grove
Tel: 305 250 9133 www.vizcayamuseum.org
Open: 9.30am–5.30pm daily

Vizcaya is the last thing you would expect to find in Miami. It's like a stately home in the heart of Europe overlooking the water,

except the water is Biscayne Bay. Built by industrialist James Deering in 1916 as his winter home, it became a museum in 1952, 27 years after his death. Inside Vizcaya boasts antiques from the 16th to the 19th centuries, as well as some of the first telephone switchboards and vacuum-cleaning systems known to man. Outside the stately gardens, pools and fountains are breathtaking. This feels a thousand miles away from South Beach.

Wolfsonian-FIU, 1001 Washington Avenue, Miami Beach
Tel: 305 531 1001   www.wolfsonian.org
Open: midday–6pm (9pm Thurs, Fri). Closed Wednesdays and holidays.

This is a small but stunning museum. Practically unique in the United States, it contains two permanent collections: the largest US display of political propaganda from the two world wars, including posters, postcards, toys and books; and an impressive collection of items from the modern era in the US and Europe

from 1885 to 1945, which concentrates on design and the relationship between man and object. A range of industrial goods and new art forms that heralded the rapid advancement of technology are also on show.

Ziff Jewish Museum, 301 Washington Avenue, South Beach
Tel: 305 672 504 www.jewishmuseum.com
Open: 10am–5pm. Closed Mondays and holidays.

A former 1936 synagogue where Miami Beach's Jewish congregation first met, the building underwent a two-year $1.5 million restoration. It is now the permanent home of MOSAIC, initially a travelling exhibition documenting the history of the Jewish community in Florida since 1763.

shop...

People in Miami love to dress up and show the world their worth, which means South Beach, in particular, has become a magnet for all the big names in fashion, as well as some talented up-and-coming designers who are spoiled for choice for models to show off their revolutionary designs.

Lincoln Road is the epicentre of South Beach activity and is full of cafés and restaurants that sprawl out onto the walkway. It's a purely pedestrian street, so a mix of shoppers, sightseers and roller-bladers share what has become the largest catwalk in Miami. As well as the restaurants, which are ideal for pit-stops, there are hundreds of shops, most of which sell women's wear.

Collins Avenue is a little more select, its shops more mainstream. The vibe is different from Lincoln Road. Instead of bars and restaurants, the shops nestle between the boutique hotels of the Art Deco district. Rather than sitting out-side a restaurant and observing the parade of shoppers, you can stop for a drink on the terrace of a hotel bar and watch the beach life slowly drift by.

Washington Avenue is a more eclectic shopping experience. The road is known for its tattoo parlours and novelty shops, but Diesel and Versace (Gianni's

house is on Ocean Drive) do their bit to add a little sparkle to a street that still hasn't quite managed to shake off the air of the drug-baron days.

For the best shopping experience in South Beach, start by walking through Collins Avenue heading north from Fifth Street (briefly popping over to Washington Avenue to Diesel and Versace) until you get to Lincoln Road where you turn left. Crucially, on South Beach, the majority of the shops stay open until around 11pm, allowing people to linger longer on the beach and still pack in some shopping and a meal.

Elsewhere, Downtown has a couple of boutique stores, but nothing really worth making the trip; the majority of the shops are budget electronic stores. The Miracle Mile in Coral Gables, however, does deserve a visit. As well as some of the best restaurants in Miami, the area boasts some high-quality stores in a more tranquil, European-looking setting. It's more relaxed here, and you don't need to dress to shop.

The serious label hunter should head north of South Beach to the Bal Harbour shops, where one finds all the names under the sun. Alternatively the Village of Merrick Park in Coral Gables is quickly coming up, with countless designers appealing to the more European sensibilities of the area. Trips to both these places aren't likely to be cheap – so break out the plastic and enjoy!

Shopping in Miami is not a pastime that's taken lightly. If you are in a rush, then make the journey to the malls, but for a real taste of Miami, and to see what's really in, go shopping on South Beach.

COLLINS AVENUE

Collins Avenue runs from the southern tip of South Beach up to Bal Harbour's malls. Although some of Miami's most exclusive hotels and restaurants can be found here, the stores sometimes don't live up to the rest of the road. After you've finished your morning's shop, pop into Robert de Niro's Ago at the Shore Club for lunch or maybe Puerto Sagua for some authentic Cuban food.

Armani – one of many upmarket designer labels; classic fashion
Banana Republic – smarter than Gap with a preppy look; would like to be Ralph Lauren
Club Monaco – clean and fresh take on mail order classics for men and women
Fitelle Paris – almost sexy, usually preppy fashion for women
Guess – denim and mid-range fashion for boys and girls
Intermix – hip fashion from Stella McCartney to the latest distressed denim
Nicole Miller – sassy and sexy clothes perfect for beach life
Polo Sport – Ralph Lauren's less exclusive brand, ideal for chilling on Ocean Drive
Quiksilver – surf's up dude! Need we say more?
Urban Outfitters – men's and women's urban apparel and accessories

LINCOLN ROAD

Lincoln Road is the spiritual home of South Beach, think hip restaurants and smart shops, all with the full accompaniment of starlets, lotharios and, of course, tourists. Stop off for a cup of coffee at Cafeteria or a long lunch at Pacific Time, or flop into a table outside Sushi Samba for a mojito and some star-spotting.

Alexa & Jack – kids' clothing with a fun and funky twist
Ann Taylor – 'meets the needs of modern woman's professional lifestyle' – hmmm…
Anthropologie – sleek, sexy and boho chic fashion with accessories and home décor to match

Base – classic SoBe offering music, books, accessories and clothes from young and fun designers

Bebe – sultry fashion for those hot SoBe summer nights

Chroma – high fashion in a little shop that's tucked away but carries up-and-coming edgy designers

En Avance – very high-end designer clothing; you even need to be buzzed in, so look the part

Fly Boutique – vintage clothing in the heart of South Beach

For Joseph – men's and women's clothing store

Galleria – high-end fashion from some top international designers from Cavalli to Ferre

I Strada – subtle clothing for women

Lucky Brand – cool, casual streetwear for men and women

Neo Accessario – a delightful range of accessories from some top names bought by even more famous clients

Neo Scarpa – exclusive and expensive shoes for men and women, owned by the same people as Neo Accessario

Palm Produce Resort Wear – Florida lifestyle clothing taken from a range of small designers

Post Blue Jean Co. – denim, denim and in case you missed it a little more denim

Rainbow – women's fashion and accessories

Soho Clothing – more fashion and accessories from the likes of Ben Sherman

Victoria's Secret – deliciously seductive lingerie and accessories

OCEAN DRIVE

Abandoned by the glitterati, Ocean Drive is now inhabited by holiday-makers clutching guidebooks. Low-end restaurants and cheap hotels play on the classic Art Deco architecture of this beach-front drive to attract tourists to their establishments. Most of the good shops have been replaced by souvenir stores.

Caterina Lucchi – Italian fashion for those who want to 'reach the highest pleasure'

WASHINGTON AVENUE

Collins Avenue's grubbier inland neighbour has a slightly grittier edge, with more low-rent stores and a down-to-earth feel. Pop into the 11th Street Diner (see Snack) for an authentic American experience pit-stop.

Belinda's – home-made clothing with a hippy twist
Cruisin' & Co. – clothes for boys and girls (think nautical, not rainbow)
Deco Collection – apparel store on SoBe
Diesel – street wear rapidly establishing itself as a classic label – close to the Diesel-inspired Pelican Hotel
Passage to India – gifts, accessories and mementos on SoBe's alternative boulevard
Santini Mavardi – slinky dresses and shoes for prowling Miami's party scene
The Shop – men's outfitters
Versace Jeans Couture – sport range from the king of bling

CLASSIC AMERICANA MALLS

Aventura Mall, 19501 Biscayne Blvd, North Miami Beach
Tel: 305 935 1110 www.shopaventuramall.com
Open: 10am–9.30pm Mon–Sat; midday–8pm Sun

2.3 million square feet of classic American brands (Victoria's Secret, Gap, Banana Republic etc.), several department stores including Bloomingdales and Macy's, a 24-screen cinema and Coco's Day Spa and Salon. It's a popular destination for families, since they organize regular events for children – your call if this is a plus point!

Cocowalk, 3015 Grand Avenue, Coconut Grove
Tel 305 444 0777 www.cocowalk.com
Open: 11am–10pm (midnight Fri, Sat) daily

A small, Mediterranean-themed shopping centre that is home to the usual high-street brands. The highlight is that it is outside and not a soulless air-conditioned shell. Visiting Brits may like to know that it actually has a Hooters.

Dolphin Mall, 11401 NW 12th Street, West Miami
Tel 305 599 3000 www.shopdolphinmall.com
Open: 10am–9.30pm Mon–Sat; 11am–7pm Sun

Mega-mall with outlet shops, attendant restaurants, cinema etc. Not the most exciting range of shops, but pretty much everyone and everything is catered for. Visit their useful website for full shop listings and current sales to decide whether or not to make the trek.

HIGH FASHION MALLS

Bal Harbour Shops, 9700 Collins Avenue, Bal Harbour
Tel: 305 866 0311 www.balharbourshops.com
Open: 10am–9pm (7pm Sat) Mon–Sat; midday–6pm Sun

High-fashion mecca, judged best shopping centre in the US by *Woman's Wear Daily*. Home to pretty much every US and European designer one might imagine: all the boys are here, from Armani to Dolce & Gabbana, Marc Jacobs, YSL, Valentino and Cavalli, to name but a few.

Village of Merrick Park, 320 San Lorenzo Avenue, Coral Gables
Tel: 305 529 0200 www.villageofmerrickpark.com
Open: 10am–9pm Mon–Sat; midday–6pm Sun

This new mall is hot contender for Bal Harbour's title. It features an eye-watering list of the cream of global fashion – from Jimmy Choo to Sonia Rykeil – and some American talent. Alleviate post-purchase remorse at the Elemis Spa (see Play).

play...

If the beach or poolside is too mundane for you, then the good news is that Miami has plenty else to offer. However, for a city with access to so much water, it is surprising how little people take to water sports in Miami – lying on the beach seems to be the main coastal activity.

That said, on Miami Beach it is possible to go jet-skiing and banana-boating (organized by the same company), but, even so, volleyball is the sport of choice (it must be something about all those oiled bodies). Dingy-sailing and kite-surfing are best enjoyed in the Key Biscayne area, south-west of South Beach.

The Miami coastline has become renowned in the scuba-diving world for attracting some of the most impressive sealife in the States. Artificial wrecks have ensured that coral has spread and that the fish, sharks and electric eels have followed.

The Miami Boat Show is one of the largest events in the city calendar, and the powerboat bug has spread, with boat owners whizzing up and down Biscayne Bay comparing engine sizes and oil spills. Alternatively, you can always charter a

yacht (which means 'powerboat' to an American, so be careful to specify whether you want your fuel to be gasoline or wind).

As for airborne thrills, there's not only parasailing but also balloon trips. It's not very Miami, but it is certainly a breathtaking experience. Otherwise helicopters can be booked, and skydiving is another option. While it's uncommon to jump

over the water and onto the beach, your pilot will nevertheless ensure that you are suitably scared and have a decent view when you are plummeting towards the earth.

The Miami Dolphins may not be the force they used to be, but this is still a football-mad town that just loves Dan Marino and its celebrity cheerleaders. If you want, you can actually learn the art of cheerleading. If you are a basketball fan, you should know that now that they have that tower of a man they call 'Shack', the Miami Heat is now regarded as one of the big guns of the NBA.

Golf is big in Florida, and Miami has its fair share of courses to choose from. Bill Clinton apparently thinks the cities' courses are fantastic, if that's anything to go by. The Biltmore Hotel is perfect for those with non-golfing partners as tennis and swimming, as well as an excellent restaurant, are on offer.

AMERICAN FOOTBALL

Miami Dolphins, 2269 Dan Marino Blvd
Tel: 305 623 6100 www.miamidolphins.com

The American Football season is played from August until February. The Dolphins last reached the playoffs in 2001, but have not won the Super Bowl since 1973. The Dolphins' stadium was the first of its kind to be constructed almost entirely of private funds totalling $115 million, and was opened in 1987 when the Chicago Bears beat the Dolphins 10–3. The last Super Bowl to be played in Miami was in 1999. Baseball's World Series was staged at the Dolphins' stadium in 1997 and 2003.

University of Miami Hurricanes, Orange Bowl Stadium, 1501 NW 3rd Street, Miami
Tel: 305 643 7100
www.ci.miami.fl.us/publicfacilities/stadiums/orange-bowl/

Formerly the Miami Dolphins' home ground, the Orange Bowl is now home to the University of Miami Hurricanes, five times national champions and NCAA record holders for college football's longest winning streak, and winners of the 2004 Orange Bowl.

BALLOON RIDES

Miami Ballooning
Tel: 305 860 5830 www.miamiballooning.com

There is not a great deal of choice when it comes to ballooning. Co-owners of Miami Ballooning, Tom Mackie and Carlos Zuniga, who used to fly balloons with balloon legend Don Caplan, dominate the market, taking clients up all year round to experience views of South Florida, the Atlantic Ocean and the Florida Everglades. Either Carlos or Tom, depending who is flying your balloon on the day, meets clients at around 5.30am and the flight commences at 6.45am. Flights last 45 minutes to an hour, and it takes 30–40 minutes to get back to the meeting point.

BASKETBALL

American Airlines Arena, 601 Biscayne Boulevard, Downtown Miami
Tel 786 777 1000 www.nba.com/heat
Season: October–April

Watch the Miami Heat play at the American Airlines Arena in Downtown Miami. The Heat, as they are known, are currently enjoying their best run in years. Tickets range from $10 to $475.

CHEERLEADING

When in Miami it is important to blend in, so why not try a spot of cheerleading? The Top Gun Cheerleading Training Centre caters for all levels.

Top Gun Cheerleading Training Centre, 13135 SW 124th Avenue, Miami
Tel: 305 259 5727 www.topguncheeranddance.com

FRISBEE

If you want to take your frisbee skills to another level, get in touch with the league in Miami, who may let you enter a team in their league as one-off.

Miami Ultimate Frisbee
Tel: 305 668 6148 www.miamiultimatefrisbee.org

GOLF

Biltmore Golf Course, 1210 Anastasia Avenue, Coral Gables, Miami
Tel: 305 460 5364 www.biltmorehotel.com

An 18-hole course forming part of the legendary Biltmore Hotel. If your partner doesn't fancy a round, there is America's largest pool and the hotel's fabulous Courtyard Grill to keep them entertained.

Crandon Park Golf Course, 6700 Crandon Boulevard, Key Biscayne
Tel: 305 361 9129 www.co.miami-dade.fl.us/parks/Parks/cran don_golf.asp
Open: 7am–6.30pm daily

The 18-hole links is one of the best public courses in Florida. It features seven saltwater lakes, mangrove thickets, sand traps – and the world's largest tee. Wow!

Miami Beach Golf Club, 2301 Alton Road, Miami Beach,
Tel: 305 532 3350 www.miamibeachgolfclub.com

Opened in 1923, this 18-holer is located in the heart of South Beach on the southern tip. Maybe pop down to Joe's Stone Crab (see Eat) for a celebratory bite after your round.

GREYHOUND RACING

Florida folk remind people that the greyhound is the oldest pure-bred dog in the world. Greyhound racing attracts a loyal following in Miami. The Hollywood Greyhound Track also has a poker room.

Flagler Dog Track, 401 NW 38th Court, Miami
Tel: 305 649 3000 www.flagerdogs.com
Open: daily June–November

Hollywood Greyhound Track, 831 North Federal Highway, Miami
Tel: 954 454 9400 www.hollywoodgreyhound.com
Open: daily December–May. Closed Mondays.

HARLEY RENTALS

Harleys are available to rent on South Beach – even such legendary models as 'Fat Boy', 'V-Rod', 'Night Train' and 'Electra Glide Classic'. The staff here will direct customers to all the Harley meets in the area. Riders must be 21 or over, must have a valid motorcycle driver's licence and hold a major credit card. Beard and bandana are optional.

American Road Collection, 1416 18th Street, Miami Beach
Tel: 305 673 8113 www.motorcyclerentals.cc
Open: 10am (9am Fri, Sat)–6pm (7pm Fri, 5pm Sat, 4pm Sun)

HELICOPTER TOURS

Hover over Miami Beach, Star Island, Brickell and Key Biscayne in Robinson helicopters. Locals use this firm to treat their children for achieving good grades at school. Hummers look surprisingly small from the air.

PHS, Kendall Tamiami Executive Airport, Miami
Tel: 305 552 8555 www.helicoptersovermiami.com

Boucher Brothers, 420 Lincoln Road #265, Miami Beach
Tel: 305 535 8177 www.boucherbrothers.com

Boucher Brothers is a full-service water-sports company that is in charge of all beach rentals on Miami Beach, including umbrellas and beach chairs. Look for the blue Boucher Brothers umbrellas to rent a jet ski on Miami Beach. The wave runners are standard class, but powerful enough to scare passengers.

Jet Ski Tours, 1416 18th Street, Miami Beach
Tel: 305 345 5770 www.jetskitoursofmiami.com

Jet Ski tours operates in the Miami Bay area, allowing clients to drive their Yamaha wave runners right past Star Island – much to the delight of the resident movie stars and rappers, who love to be pried on. Dolphins have allegedly been seen in the bay area, as have salt-water crocodiles.

KITE-BOARDING

Miami Kite Boarding, Rickenbacker Causeway, Key Biscayne
Tel: 305 345 9974 www.miamikiteboarding.com

Kite-boarding, or kite-surfing as we call it this side of the Pond, takes place at Key Biscayne, a 15-minute drive from South Beach. Classes are available for first-timers, and surfers will be taken to shallow sandbars to improve take-offs before being allowed to go and play with the sharks and manta rays.

LIMO RENTALS

There is nothing like a Hummer limo to turn heads in Miami. With fully stocked bars and entertainment systems inside, there is no real reason to get out of one's Hummer limo, unless you want to go to a nightclub or bar to recruit more limo lovers.

A1 Limousine, 6177 Jog Road Site, Lake Worth
Tel: 561 964 7764 www.a1limobus.com

LUXURY CAR RENTALS

There are no two ways about it: boys in Miami believe that flash
cars and fat wallets impress girls on South Beach. And judging by
the number of attractive girls being driven around in Ferraris by
greasy, unattractive boys, you'd have to admit that they have a
point. So if you are even vaguely good-looking, just think how
many pretty girls will think you are a superstar with a fat wallet
if you rent a souped-up Lamborghini for the evening. Some of
them might even hop in for a ride. Remember to drive very
slowly, rest your left elbow on the open window and rev up the
engine to at least 6,000rpm when driving down Collins Avenue;
then turn around.

Dream Exotic
Tel: 866 293 9061 www.hotcarsmiami.com

Excellence Luxury Car Rental, 3851 Bird Road, Miami
Tel: 305 526 0000 www.excellenceluxury.com

Luxury Rent a Car
Tel: 305 794 2017 www.lapcr.com

PAINTBALLING

Ruff N Tuff Paintball, 13200 NW 43rd Avenue
Tel: 305 953 7776 www.ruffntuffpaintball.com

Paintballing is an official sport and the set-up at Ruff N Tuff is
extremely professional; it's run by Peter Bofill, who has over 20
years' experience in the game. Clients can shoot at each other

on three different battlegrounds: the woods, for the jungle warfare lover; the Hyperball; and the Lego fields for those more partial to guerrilla warfare.

PARASAILING

Captain Bob's Parasail, Loews Hotel, Ocean Drive, Miami Beach
Tel: 305 266 4144

This is the only parasailing company on South Beach, and its parachute, 800 feet in the air, can be seen all along the beach. Look for a blue Boucher Brothers umbrella close to the water. The captain and his team will send you up in pairs or alone. From above, parasailors often see sharks patrolling the Miami coastline and manta rays gliding through the shallow water. The view of the Beach is spectacular, but the journey out to sea can be a little unnerving when the parachute begins to creak in the wind. An experience not to be missed.

SCUBA-DIVING

Tarpoon Lagoon, 300 Alton Road, Miami Beach
Tel: 305 532 1445 www.tarpoondivecentre.com

Ships have been purposefully sunk along the Miami coast in order to encourage coral growth in the area. The results have been spectacular as divers around the world come to get a glimpse of eagle-rays, nurse sharks, green and spotted moray eels and barracuda, among other species. Beginners can do a four-day course before attempting their first dive in the ocean. Tarpoon organizes both daytime and noctural dives. Monty's Bar (see Drink) is located beside the shop.

SKY-DIVING

Sky Dive Miami, 28730 SW 217th Avenue, Homestead
Tel: 305 759 3483 www.skydivemiami.com

Sky Dive Miami jumps with over a thousand first-timers each year. Jumps are from over two miles high and, like everywhere in Miami, reservations are necessary. Full-minute tandem diving is available (13,500 feet), and jumps can be filmed on request.

SPAS

Agua Bathhouse Spa, Delano Hotel
Tel: 800 949 7414 www.delanohotelmiamibeach.com
Open: 9am–7pm daily, women only; 7.30–11pm Wed–Mon, men only

Located on the Delano's roof, the renovated Agua Bathhouse offers a full range of massages, including classics like the Deep Tissue massage, the Aromatherapy Treatment, the Table Shiatsu, and the Custom Swedish massage. Also on the menu are meditation, body treatments such as the Rosemary and Cedarwood body scrub, the Ocean Rose body scrub, all kinds of facials, manicures, pedicures and hair treatments.

Elemis Spa, 330 Avenue San Lorenzo, 2345 Village of Merrick Park, Coral Gables
Tel: 305 774 7171 www.elemis.com/usa/miami.html
Open: 9am (10am Sun)–9pm (8pm Fri/Sat, 6pm Sun) daily

The Elemis spa goes all-out on its facials, incorporating all sorts of oriental treatments such as the Japanese Silk Booster facial or the Age Zone treatment. Elemis offers all the run-of-the-mill massages, but adds a few into the mixer such as the Hawaiian Wave Four Hand massage. Perhaps the most attractive option is the Lovers' Ritual, which includes massage classes for lovers before the pampering sessions begin.

Mandarin Oriental Hotel, 500 Brickell Key Drive, Downtown
Tel: 305 913 833 www.mandarinoriental.com
Open: 9.30am–9.30pm daily

The Mandarin Oriental's award-winning spa is a tri-level sanctuary featuring 17 treatment rooms, six of which overlook Biscayne Bay, a fitness centre and a yoga room. Signature treatments include Ayurvedic holistic body treatment, Life Dance, Balinese synchronized massage, Thai massage, the Mandarin hot stone therapy and the Mandarin oriental luxury facial.

Ritz Carlton South Beach, 1 Lincoln Road, Miami Beach
Tel: 786 276 4090 www.ritzcarlton.com
Open: 9am–7pm daily

The Ritz Carlton's spa covers 16,000 square feet, has 14 treatment rooms and is particularly pleased with its 'Power Shower' with 23 body sprays. This spa's signature treatments include the Après SoBe, which is the French Floridonian way of saying hangover cure; the Carita Avant SoBe, which is the Spa's way of preparing you for a big night out on South Beach; and the SoBe Privé, which is a six-hour treatment that enlivens all the five senses.

The Spa at the Setai, 2001 Collins Avenue, Miami Beach
Tel: 305 520 6900 www.setai.com
Open: 8am–9pm daily

Along with the Mandarin Oriental's spa, the Setai offers an oriental take on how to pamper people. The Setai's spa is rather smaller and more personal than its competitors, and is situated in a two-storey building beside the pool area. Massage treatments include the Himalayan hot stone massage and Balinese massage, as well as signature bath rituals such as the China Sea uplifting bath or the Malaysian Rainforest relaxing bath.

The Standard, 40 island Avenue, Miami Beach
Tel: 305 673 1717 www.standardhotel.com

The Standard Hotel's entire property is based around the spa, which draws influence from treatments from around the world encouraging 'bathing' as a social practice. Hence the Turkish-style Hammam and scrub room, the Roman Waterfall hot-tub, Arctic plunge pool, aroma steam room and cedar sauna. Mud baths, spa treatment rooms, a skincare clinic, holistic massage therapies as well as yoga classes make this the ultimate healthy retreat from South Beach. The wholesome restaurant nourishes the stomach while the garden fire lounge will get you in the mood to tackle another evening on the beach.

SWIMMING POOLS

Alongside Miami's hotel architecture, the swimming pools have become features in their own right. The Raleigh's is probably the most beautiful in town, but others come close to the mark. The pools listed here aren't public pools but if you arrived changed and spend money at the pool bar the hotel's don't seem to mind you having a quick dip. Normally open from 8am to 9pm.

The Biltmore, 1210 Anastasia Avenue, Coral Gable
Tel: 305 445 1926 www.biltmorehotel.com
Open: 5.30am (7am Sat/Sun)–10pm (9pm Fri–Sun)

In the era of aquatic shows, the Biltmore's pool staged water ballets and water polo matches. Like most public pools, the diving boards have now been converted into water features, but it is still legal to attempt to swim a length under water. It has been done, apparently. Oh, and by the way, the pool is the largest in the United States.

The Hotel, 801 Collins Avenue, South Beach
Tel: 305 531 2222 www.thehotelofsouthbeach.com

The Hotel's rooftop pool is not really taken advantage of by The Hotel's guests, so is idyllic for appreciating the view of the Atlantic Ocean and Miami Beach in peace. The sun beds are simple but, decent and there is a poolside bar with full service. This pool is ideal for simultaneous wading and cocktail drinking, and is magnificent for a late-night dip. Unfortunately guests only, but a good place for a drink.

Raleigh, 1775 Collins Avenue, South Beach
Tel: 305 534 6300 www.raleighhotel.com

This landscaped lagoon pool, heralded as a jewel of modernist
design, is the most famous of all the pools in Miami and has
appeared in many a movie. Unfortunately, what was one the best
diving-boards on the beach has now become a water feature, but
visitors can be comforted by the fact that the Raleigh Hotel's
weekly pool party on a Sunday afternoon is without doubt the
coolest opportunity you will be afforded to show off your six-
pack. The pool bar is an altar-like feature at the corner of the
pool, beside which a DJ spins. By nightfall the pool area and the
hotel's enclosed beach (which is where the water used to reach
before the beach was re-laid) becomes a party zone. The monthly full-moon parties are fun too.

Shore Club, 1901 Collins Avenue, South Beach
Tel: 305 695 3277 www.shoreclubmiamibeach.com

Along with the Raleigh, the Shore Club attracts beautiful people,
making what is a square, minimalist tub of water into a decadent
oasis of fun. Surrounding the main pool are bed-like sun-loungers
that are meant to be shared and are the most comfortable
within a mile radius. This area gets busy in the evenings when the
Sky Bar fills up, which can disturb guests who are after a relaxing
drink by the pool.

TENNIS

The 12-day annual NASDAQ-100 Open starts mid-March and is
one of the biggest non-Grand Slam events in the world. Otherwise tennis courts are few and far between on South Beach, but
there are a few on the Miami mainland, usually in private clubs.

Biltmore Tennis, 1210 Anastasia Avenue, Coral Gables
Tel: 305 460 5360 www.biltmorehotel.com

Part of the enormous Biltmore Hotel complex – while you get sweaty with the tennis pro you can always send your husband off for a round of golf. Then innocently meet for a delicious lunch at the hotel's Courtyard Grill (see Snack).

Brickell Tennis Club, 601 South Miami Avenue, Brickell
Tel: 305 858 3375 www.cliffdrysdale.com/brickell

State-of-the-art tennis club offering seven courts. With typical efficiency, attendants are on hand to offer fresh towels and cold drinks.

Crandon Park Tennis Center, 7300 Crandon Boulevard, Key Biscayne
Tel: 305 446 2400 www.nasdaq-100open.com

Home of the aforementioned NASDAQ-100. Is this a chance to see 'Tiger' Tim Henman under-perform again? Failing that, the boys can hope for a glimpse of Maria Sharapova.

YACHT CHARTERS

Powerboats are very popular in Miami. In fact, many Miami locals say that their powerboats say more about their personality than their car. The bay area is popular for cruising, but a trip along South Beach is always a tempting option and is a good chance to effect that *Baywatch*-style rescue by saving a damsel in distress.

Florida Yacht, 390 Alton Road, Suite 3 Miami Beach
Tel: 305 532 8600 www.floridayacht.com

Sailing Yachts (Hunter 460s, Hunter 450 Center Cockpits, Hunter 410s). Weekly rates $2,400–4,100.

Catamarans (Leopard 45 Catamaran, Lagoon 410 Catamaran, Lagoon 380 Catamaran). Weekly rates $3,600–5,500.

Motor Yachts (Mainship 430 Trawlers, Mainship 350 Trawlers, FP Maryland 37 Power Cat. Weekly rates $3,300–5,500.

info...

CLIMATE

In the winter, January and February, the average temperatures are between 13°C and 15°C. Apart from winter, the climate in Miami only varies slightly and remains constantly warm. Average summer temperatures in June, July, August and September are between 25°C and 30°C. A cool ocean breeze helps keep the temperature down and gives the beach a refreshing edge. Do remember to use sun block at all times.

DRESS

If you want to look the part, it's time to fish your best garments out of the wardrobe and take out your life savings. Think cutting-edge fashion with a slutty edge to it (because of the heat, of course) and you'll get how people dress in Miami. Jeans are allowed if they are ripped in the right places, but long dresses are unheard of, and trainers or 'sneakers' are not welcome unless you are famous or they really do go with your outfit. Wearing a jacket can help men to get into lounges, and wife-beaters (sleeveless T-shirts) and sunglasses are what the die-hard clubber wears on a rave night.

DRUGS

Miami has a reputation for being the pharmacy of the south for narcotics lovers, but drugs are frowned on and there are always undercover cops keeping an eye out for dealers and consumers, especially in the more high-profile clubs. One serious point to take in is that girls should be extremely careful in Miami with what is known as the 'date rape' drug Rohypnol, which is colourless, odourless, tasteless and dissolves in drinks without leaving any trace. There are many tales of girls having the drug slipped into their cocktails and not remembering anything the next day. So be careful who buys your drinks and never leave your glass unattended. This also applies to men – remember that this is a gay town too. Will you be offered drugs? In lounge clubs you will probably not be offered anything but alcohol, but in large downtown clubs drugs (mainly ecstacy and cocaine) may well be on offer.

GETTING IN

The Miami bouncer holds the key to the party, so be nice to him, but not too nice so that he thinks you are soft. His requirements are primarily money and also good looks, but neither, however, is any good without a hint of self-belief and arrogance. In Miami it is perfectly acceptable to believe that you are a multi-millionaire or a model. If you do not know the right people, look the part or arrive flanked by long-legged blondes, then get your concierge to have your name added to the guest list, arrive early and make sure that you are looking as good as you possibly can, otherwise the velvet ropes will not be lowered for you — ever.

TAXIS

Miami cabs make New York taxis look cheap. The dire public transport system in Miami means that, if you haven't rented a car, taking a cab is the only option. Taxi firms are well aware of this and the cabs' fare meters move faster than the second hand of a clock. A taxi from the airport to South Beach is roughly $30, as is a taxi from South Beach to Downtown.

TIPPING

The cost of your holiday just went up by 20 per cent. Waiters, waitresses and bar tenders don't earn a proper wage, so they rely on tips as their sole source of income. Tipping, therefore, is a must otherwise nobody will serve you. In Miami you are supposed to tip in taxis, bars, nightclubs and even when you dry your hands outside the 'restroom' — basically at every opportunity. On South Beach it is common for the bill to have an extra 18 per cent added onto it for service. This is because Europeans do not usually tip, so the restaurant takes the liberty of adding on the gratuity. You can, however, refuse to pay it if you think the service is not up to scratch. In bars, be sure to tip after every drink you buy. Usually $1 or $2 per drink is seen as adequate. Bar tenders will begin to overlook you if your tipping slows down.